The Spellmount Siegfried Line Series

Ardennes: The Secret War

ARDENNES: THE SECRET WAR

by

Charles Whiting

SPELLMOUNT
Staplehurst

British Library Cataloguing in Publication Data:
A catalogue record for this book is available
from the British Library

Copyright © Charles Whiting 1984, 2001

ISBN 1-86227-120-8

First published in 1984 by Century Publishing Co Ltd
This edition first published in the UK in 2001 by
Spellmount Limited
The Old Rectory
Staplehurst
Kent TN12 0AZ

Tel: 01580 893730
Fax: 01580 893731
E-mail: enquiries@spellmount.com
Website: www.spellmount.com

1 3 5 7 9 8 6 4 2

The right of Charles Whiting to be identified
as the author of this work has been asserted by him
in accordance with the Copyright, Designs
and Patents Act 1988

Printed in Great Britain by
T.J. International, Padstow, Cornwall

Contents

BOOK ONE
AUTUMN FOG*

But if Intelligence was not to blame, who was?
General K. Strong, Eisenhower's Chief-of-Intelligence

---

* '*Herbstnebel*', the first code-name of the great surprise offensive

THE BACKGROUND
Saturday, 16 December 1944

On that grey, gloomy December Saturday forty years ago now when their world fell apart, the Top Brass played. If at the front on Germany's snowbound western border the millions of soldiers, British, French, Canadian and American, under their command fought and perhaps died that day, they played. After all it was a *Saturday*, wasn't it?

The Englishman Montgomery, in command of the British Twenty-first Army Group, flew from his headquarters to the golf links at the Dutch town of Eindhoven for a few holes of golf with Welsh golf pro Dai Rees. His greatest rival, the American Bradley, the lantern-jawed commander of the US Eighteenth Army Group, met with his subordinate commanders, Generals Hodges and Quesada of the Army Air Corps in Spa, Belgium. In Hodges' office at the Hôtel Britannique, where in 1918 Field Marshal 'Papa' von Hindenburg had told his crippled Kaiser that the war was lost for imperial Germany, the Belgian gunmaker, Monsieur Francotte, fitted the three Americans up for their custom-made shotguns.

Further south at Nancy in France, America's most flamboyant commander, General 'Blood an' Guts' Patton, ate a leisurely breakfast in the mess. He knew it was against his own specific order for an officer to eat breakfast later than seven-thirty, but he had attended a conference at six-thirty that morning, where there had been some desultory discussion of unusual troop movements on the German side of the line. So he felt justified in breaking his own rule; and after all, this was the start of the weekend, the last one before Christmas, as well.

1

Far to the rear at Versailles, their boss the Supreme Commander, General Eisenhower, known to half the world as 'Ike' by now, took it easy, too. In the 5,000-strong head-quarters, most of the staff were still asleep. Not Ike's family, though. Kay Summersby, his green-eyed British secretary–mistress; 'Butch', his hearty 'life-of-the-party' PR man; 'Tex', who kept his records; even Telek, the pet dog – they were all up, for there was excitement in the air this Saturday morning. After a leisurely breakfast, Ike read a letter from Montgomery. The cocky little Englishman, with the beaky nose and fierce unwinking blue eyes, had written to request Christmas leave to be in England with his only son whom he had not seen since before the invasion six months earlier. With the letter there was a marker, reminding Eisenhower that fourteen months earlier he had bet a fiver that the war would be over by Christmas 1944.

'I still have nine days,' Eisenhower would write back, enjoying the little private joke, happy that for once the 'pesky little Britisher' wasn't making one of his usual categoric demands. Christmas was coming; everyone seemed to be in a much more relaxed, tolerant mood, even 'Monty'. Later, after it had all happened, Eisenhower would bitterly regret that he had ever written that bantering little reply. It would show just how complacent he and all the rest of the Top Brass had been on that December Saturday.

Just after ten o'clock, Eisenhower and most of his staff went across to the Louis XIV chapel at Versailles. There they attended the wedding of ex-bellhop Mickey McKeogh, his valet, who Ike was convinced brought him luck, and the diminutive, bespectacled WAC* sergeant Pearlie Hargrave. It was the democratic thing to do. Besides, it made for good public relations, and General Eisenhower had long learned the need to cultivate the all-powerful US press.

Later Eisenhower gave a reception for the happy young couple – and the champagne flowed liberally. Indeed, Kay Summersby would record one day later when her lover's

---

*US Women's Army Corps

divisions were reeling back in scared confusion on that remote front, that 'half of headquarters was soggy with the silence of plain, unadulterated, ordinary hangovers!'

Eisenhower had another and personal reason for celebrating this last happy Saturday; he had just heard he had been nominated by Congress for the newly created rank of 'General of the Army', which carried five stars. Now he had really achieved the status of old 'Black Jack' Pershing, who had commanded US troops in Europe in the Old War when Eisenhower had been a lowly captain in charge of guarding strategic installations and training troops back in the States. Now, although he had never fired a shot in anger or commanded even a company in action, he was America's most powerful 'fighting' soldier in the European theatre! It was a heady feeling.

At the reception he was button-holed by an old crony, a graduate from West Point like himself, hard-drinking, skirt-chasing General Everett Hughes. Hughes wasn't there for Sergeant Pearlie Hargrave's sake; he was there to congratulate Ike. He told his boss happily, 'I couldn't bear the idea of having gotten drunk when you received the fourth star and not having a drink with you on your fifth.'

Ike gave Hughes the benefit of that ear-to-ear smile that had become famous to cinema audiences all over the Western world in these last twelve months and invited his old crony over for dinner that night. 'Brad' – Bradley – was coming over to spend the weekend. This afternoon they'd have a chat about the shortage of riflemen at the front. That night they'd have a comfy, all-male dinner party, just like in the old days before the war.

Hughes thanked Ike and said he'd be there. He'd bring a bottle of Highland Piper scotch. In Hughes' eyes there could be no deeper mark of respect, in a Supreme Headquarters, swamped in bourbon, captured German *Kognak* and French champagne, but chronically short of good scotch!

For that evening, Eisenhower's 'darkies', as the Supreme Commander still called his black mess servants, had prepared a special treat. A well-wisher had presented him with a bushel of oysters, which Ike adored. The 'darkies' were preparing oysters on the half-shell as an entrée, to be followed by oyster stew, with fried oysters concluding the festive meal.*

At two o'clock the replacement conference started in the Map Room at Versailles. Outside it was bitterly cold. Inside it was pleasantly warm, and the six officers present, having eaten a large lunch, took their time. The problem wasn't particularly urgent. Nothing much was currently happening at the front, which seemed, almost everywhere, to have settled for a dreary winter sleep. There would be no victory in Europe by this Christmas, that was for sure.

Now outside, it was already beginning to darken, when the most junior officer present, the British Brigadier Kenneth Strong, Eisenhower's Chief-of-Intelligence, noted that his deputy, US Brigadier-General Betts, was at the door.

Betts was normally a calm, phlegmatic man. Now he seemed to tall, dark-haired Scot Ken Strong to be shaken. He frowned and rose to see what the trouble was. Hastily Betts passed Strong a note. He read it and then interrupted the conference to read aloud the message that Betts had brought: 'This morning the enemy counter-attacked at five separate points across the First Army sector!'

Bradley surmised that it was merely a spoiling attack; he had already heard there was some trouble at the front while he had been at Hodges' headquarters. All the time the three generals were being measured up for their shotguns, aides had been bringing in messages about enemy penetrations of Hodges' First Army's positions. He wasn't too worried.

'This is no local attack, Brad,' Eisenhower said. 'It isn't logical for the Germans to launch a local attack at our weakest point.'

'If it's not a local attack,' Bradley retorted unperturbed, 'what kind of an attack is it?'

'That remains to be seen,' Eisenhower said. 'But I don't think we can afford to sit on our hands till we've found out.'

---

* In the event, Brad was found to hate oysters. He had to be satisfied with hastily prepared scrambled eggs. Forty years later, one wonders what staff officer got a 'rocket' for that oversight!

It was decided to alert two divisions to stand by to help Hodges, one of them coming from Patton's Third Army.

'I suppose,' Bradley said, 'that it *would* be safer that way. Of course, you know one of these divisions will have to come from Patton.'

'So?' Eisenhower said.

'So. Georgie won't like losing a division a few days before his big attack on the Saar.'

'You tell him,' Eisenhower snorted, 'that Ike is running this damned war!'

Thereafter the conference adjourned for the great oyster dinner, while away at Spa, Hodges, whose HQ would be in full flight within the next forty-eight hours, frantically tried to call Eisenhower or Bradley. In vain. For already the Germans had begun cutting the land lines; and who knows, perhaps Hughes' prized Highland Piper was beginning to have its celebrated effect?

On that Saturday, 16 December 1944, when the great German offensive commenced that was going to cost the Americans 77,000 men killed, wounded, missing or taken prisoner and the British another 1,500, the Top Brass was taken completely off guard. The fact that two huge tank armies, some 600,000 men in all, had been assembled under their very noses was a scandal of the first water: one that was hushed up at the time by means of a forty-eight-hours' news blackout in the West and subsequently by doctoring the relevant documents. Even Strong, Eisenhower's Chief-of-Intelligence, did not know, until nearly twenty-five years later, that there had been a secret investigation into the security slip-up at the time; and to his very death, he could not explain just how both file copies of the relevant intelligence summaries for that week, one kept in London and the other at Versailles, were destroyed. Personally, I don't think one needs a crystal ball to know why.

That winter, when the Top Brass thought that Hitler's vaunted 'Thousand-year Reich' was virtually on its knees, the Germans achieved a surprise which must be ranked with the most brilliant of the wartime Anglo-American deception operations, such as 'Bodyguard', 'Fortitude'* and the 'Double-Cross System'† and all the rest of those intelligence coups of which the British, in particular, were – and are – so proud.

From October till December 1944 the Germans had been able to assemble and train a massive attack force of three armies, not on the other side of the twenty-three-mile broad Channel, as had been the case with the Allies before June 1944, but a mere two hundred yards or so away on the other side of the front line!

Furthermore, with a handful of German parachutists dropped behind Allied lines and the use of long-range jeep teams, not more than a dozen in number, their crews speaking fluent English and dressed in US uniforms, the German High Command was able to start an unprecedented spy scare. Just as in May 1940, the scare spread from the front throughout the Allied armies, and from them to the civilian populations of France, Belgium, Holland and Luxembourg. Once again the long refugee columns started rolling westwards, and everywhere civilian police were looking for – and finding – German parachutists dressed in that classic garb of the German infiltrator, known to every village gendarme since 1940, that of an innocent nun! Alarm did not even stop there, but crossed the Channel to Britain, with rumours abounding that there were to be mass breakouts from German POW camps. The POWs, released thus and armed with weapons paradropped to them or taken from their surprised guards, would then seize key ports in the South-east in order to facilitate enemy landings in the United Kingdom. This time Operation 'Sea Lion'‡ would really take place!

The consequence of this great scare that virtually paralysed the rear areas of the Allied front in Europe was that 'half a million GIs played cat-and-mouse with each other', as an irate

---

*Pre-D-Day intelligence deceptions to confuse the Germans on the Allied landing sites.

†The scheme to 'turn' all German spies captured in the UK in World War II and make them work for British intelligence.

‡German code-name for the planned invasion of the UK in 1940

General Bradley put it. Everywhere strangers in US uniform were stopped, asked passwords, riddles, popular US catch-phrases of the day – 'Who's Betty Grable's husband?', 'Who's dem bums' and so on – in order to ascertain whether they were genunine or not. Even generals, including General Bradley, were held up in this fashion. Some were even arrested by their own MPs. General Bruce Clarke of the 7th US Armoured Division was one such unfortunate. And as for the Supreme Commander himself, once the rumour reached Versailles that he was to be assassinated by German para-commandos disguised as Americans, he was held a virtual prisoner by his own troops. For five crucial days while the Germans pushed ever westwards, threatening to split the American and British army groups from one another and cut them off from the key supply port of Antwerp, Eisenhower fumed impotently in his own HQ, over 120 miles from the front. In that time he was guarded by tanks and a whole battalion of heavily armoured MPs, forbidden to leave the confines of the headquarters compound. Even when he was allowed to go to his office, two hundred yards away from his quarters, he was driven by an armed officer in a closed jeep, which was escorted by a company of MPs, armed with tommy-guns, and armoured cars! Even the President of the United States himself in a security-conscious United States had never merited such overwhelming security precautions.

That dark December of the last Christmas of the war, the Germans pulled off a tremendous intelligence coup. Never before had they been able to do anything like it – and they would never do it again. The Top Brass had been caught napping. Later they made frantic efforts to re-establish their reputations. No episode in the whole course of the war caused so much public polemic, personal vituperation and self-vindication. They attempted to show that they had expected the attack in the Ardennes; hadn't been fooled at all; had taken that 'calculated risk' that Top Brass was always talking about, a risk that was never apparent to the soldiers who had to pay the 'butcher's bill'.

Nevertheless, the verdicts of both the US and British official histories still stand. Hugh M. Cole, the American official historian, wrote: 'Sentences, phrases and punctuation marks from American intelligence documents of pre-Ardennes origin have been twisted and turned, noted in and out of context, *interpreted* and misinterpreted, in arduous efforts to fix blame and secure absolution.' The British official history stated: 'The well-kept secret of what had been going on behind the German scene was largely undiscovered or misunderstood by Allied Intelligence and so *not anticipated by Allied commanders*' (my italics). But in the end, in spite of the bluster, the name-calling, the passing of blame to others, there was no denying the fact that the enemy had well and truly surprised the generals.

This then, seen from the German side of the line, is the story of the greatest surprise that the Wehrmacht was able to spring on the complacent Western Allies during the course of their campaign in Europe in that dark December of forty years ago. It is a tale of self-deception, double-dealing and, in the end, sudden death.

It is not a pleasant story. No story is pleasant which details just how wilfully and carelessly young lives were thrown away. But then in those grim days which led up to the last Christmas of World War II, when so many men, American, British and German, fought and died, there were few pleasant stories.

ONE
Three Colonels

1

Dawn, 16 October 1944.

Above the waiting men, puffing silently at their last cigarettes, the stark outline of the castle which housed the traitor was silhouetted against the dirty white sky. In front of them lay the Wienerstrasse, the winding steep road they would take soon. It was silent and empty. But the smoking soldiers in the black uniforms of the *Panzertruppe* and the camouflaged coveralls of the SS knew that meant nothing. For all they knew it was mined and barricaded, with Hungarian soldiers positioned in the buildings on both sides, just waiting for them to walk straight into a trap.

Up front the SS giant with the scarred face rose in his Volkswagen jeep, towering above his bodyguard of five noncoms, hung with stick grenades and extra mags for their machine pistols. His force seemed very small for the task ahead of them. Four tanks; a troop of Goliaths, miniature remote-controlled tracked vehicles, each packing 500 pounds of high explosive; and two companies of parachute infantry. But it was all that was available to him to capture the fortified complex, the Burgberg,* reputedly held by a whole Hungarian division, and capture the traitor, who was now about to betray the Führer and take Hungary out of the war on Germany's side.

---

* Castle Hill

The risk was terribly high. Yet the SS giant knew he was in need of a victory in this terrible autumn, 1944. Ever since he had snatched Mussolini, the Italian dictator, from underneath the very noses of his captors and his name had flashed round the world (even Churchill had praised him in the House of Commons), his plans for similar triumphs had been thwarted time and time again. And what bold ventures they had all been! A paradrop on Baku to blow up the Red army's main source of oil; the destruction by his *Kampfschwimmer** of the Suez Canal installations so that the British could not use the Mediterranean; a kamikaze bombing raid on the House of Commons to kill Churchill; an aerial bombardment of New York by the new V-1 and V-2 missiles carried by submarine across the Atlantic. . . . Yet events had always overtaken his tremendous schemes and made them impossible to execute. Now, however, it was different. Now he would capture the traitor Horthy, keep the Hungarian army in the war as germany's ally, and save the lives of one million German soldiers who would be surely swamped by the Red army on Hungary's eastern frontier if that country surrendered.

The SS giant looked at his most prized possession, a gold watch given to him by Mussolini, on its back a Napoleonic initial 'M', with the date of the rescue inscribed on it: '12.9.43'. 'Mussolini time', he always joked when asked the time by his comrades. It was exactly one minute to six. Hurriedly his men sprang aboard their vehicles. Motors burst into noisy life. Rudely the morning stillness was shattered by drivers gunning their cold engines. The air was full of the stink of diesel fumes. SS Major Otto Skorzeny, the scar-faced giant, touched his Knight's Cross at his throat won for rescuing the Duce, as if to reassure himself, and then barked above the racket, '*Los . . . Vorwärts!*' His driver thrust home first. The little jeep moved forward. Behind, the rest of the tense column followed. The bold strike had begun. Operation '*Panzerfaust*'† was under way.

---

* Battle swimmers, i.e. frogmen
† Operation 'Bazooka'

The man who had rescued Mussolini from his mountain fortress and was now head of the SS commandos had arrived in Budapest, the Hungarian capital, a few days earlier disguised – very implausibly for such a dangerous-looking man – as a Herr Doktor Wolf, a German tourist, armed with an ancient Baedeker guide, to do the sights. In fact, he was spying out the layout of the Burgberg, which housed the seat of the Hungarian government, and observing the antics of the Hungarian dictator's favourite son, Miklos 'Miki' Horthy.

Miki was the *enfant terrible* of the dictator's family. He ran a stable of mistresses and threw wild parties; but still he was the apple of the dictator's eye, more especially now since Admiral Horthy's older son Istvan, a pilot, had been killed on the Russian front. Now the playboy had become a politician, negotiating the surrender of Germany's ally Hungary to the Russians, by way of representatives of the Yugoslav partisan chief, Tito.

In the end Skorzeny, alias Dr Wolf, decided that the best way to keep Admiral Horthy in the war was to use his darling son, Miki, as a hostage. It was agreed with the local Gestapo, who were covering the clandestine meetings, that the next time the playboy met the Yugoslavs, he was to be kidnapped and spirited away to Germany; it was the kind of decisive stroke, using small numbers, which always appealed to Skorzeny. It was a sparkling, quiet autumn Sunday morning when Dr Wolf drove up to the square outside the house where Miki had his next meeting with the Yugoslavs. The place seemed empty save for two Hungarian lorries parked outside the meeting place. A little further there was a canvas-backed Hungarian army lorry and Miki's private limousine.

Wolf parked and pretended to fiddle under the hood of his car. Across the way the canvas hood was jerked back to see what was going on, and Skorzeny caught a quick glimpse of a heavy machine gun, manned by three Hungarian soldiers. The traitors had come prepared for trouble. Soon they were going to get it!

A couple of German MPs strolled into the square. It seemed as if they were on a routine patrol. Suddenly, however, they lost their air of casual unconcern. Before anyone could stop them, they darted towards the building where the conspirators were meeting. The Hungarians flung back the canvas. The machine gun chattered. One of the policemen slammed to the cobbles, hit. Skorzeny darted forward, slugs cutting the air all around him. He grabbed the policeman by the collar and dragged him panting to safety.

Hungarian soldiers started to stream into the square. Now Skorzeny's men rushed out of cover to meet them. Skorzeny's driver was hit. The rest of his men took up the Hungarian challenge with their pistols. But the Hungarian machine gun was too much for them. Soon, Skorzeny knew, his men would be overrun. He rose and blew a shrill blast on his whistle. Almost immediately his main body, the SS commandos, under the command of his adjutant, Baron von Foelkersam, came pelting up the street towards the square, firing as they came.

The sight took the heart out of the Hungarians. They started to back off. Skorzeny didn't wait for them to recover. At the head of his men he ran for it, his SS paras throwing stick grenades to left and right wildly as they darted towards the house. Above them on the roof, Hungarian soldiers started to rip up bricks and pieces of marble to shower them with. But the unusual weapons did not stop Skorzeny's men. Within minutes they were inside, panting and flushed with victory, to find that the Germans already planted in the building had captured young Horthy and were holding him at pistol point.

The playboy, flushed and angry, was waving his hands and threatening a terrible revenge on his abductors. Skorzeny had no time to waste on him and didn't want to use physical violence on his precious hostage. His gaze flashed around the apartment. His eyes fell on a large flowered carpet, then on a thick piece of curtain-rope at the french window. Swiftly he rapped out an order. Without ceremony, the protesting playboy was flung on the floor, wrapped in the carpet and trussed securely like an animal being readied for the market.

'To the airfield.' Skorzeny cried. 'I'll follow!' He turned to von Foelkersam. 'And no more shooting, understood?'

Baron von Foelkersam grinned and nodded. Together they

left the apartment. The whole of Operation 'Mickey Mouse', as it was later called, had taken exactly ten minutes The question now was: how would Admiral Horthy react?

While Skorzeny chain-smoked nervously at his Budapest hotel HQ and waited, the Hungarians reacted. Up on the hill, the Burgberg, Horthy's residence, was completely sealed off. Heavily armed troops dug in everywhere. All roads were barricaded. Even minefields were laid hurriedly.

Then Radio Budapest cut into its normal programmes. The speaker announced that the nation should stand by for an important announcement by Admiral Horthy at two o'clock that afternoon. Together with his officers and an interpreter Skorzeny stood by. The ageing admiral began promptly at two o'clock with an angry tirade against his erstwhile ally. Germany, he declared firmly, had lost the war. Finally he made his position quite clear. Although he had suppressed the Communist government of 1919 in Hungary in a bloody massacre, he now intended to make a separate peace with the 'red beast'. Already he had asked for an armistice. Hostilities between the Russians and the Hungarians would cease at once! Skorzeny had gambled and failed. The daring kidnapping scheme had come to naught. Thus Operation 'Bazooka' was born.

Slowly the SS convoy rolled up the Wienerstrasse towards the fortifications. Next to Skorzeny, von Foelkersam whispered, 'Bit unpleasant if we were hit by fire from the flank, Major, eh?'

Skorzeny didn't answer. His heart was thudding. Any moment he expected to hit one of the mines that reportedly had been planted in the approach road. But nothing happened.

'Go a little faster,' he hissed to his driver, and pumped his arm up and down several times rapidly to indicate to the drivers behind him that they should do the same.

Things were going well. Sentries appeared from the shadows. Skorzeny waved to them cheerfully. The Hungarians clicked to attention. Behind Skorzeny's jeep, his tank commanders in their turrets saluted stiffly. Skorzeny breathed a sigh. They were through the first barrier!

Now they were rolling toward Horthy's residence at twenty miles an hour. The entrance was only about a thousand yards away. Three Hungarian tanks were parked inside. The column continued. Would the Hungarians fire? Suddenly the first tank raised its 75mm. cannon high into the air, an indication that it would not fire. Seconds later they had rolled past them. A barricade loomed up. Skorzeny signalled the Panther tank immediately behind him to take action. At top speed it crashed into the barricade. It disintegrated – to reveal six manned anti-tank guns positioned behind it!

Skorzeny didn't wait to see what would happen. '*Los!*' he roared and sprang out of the jeep, followed by his bodyguard and von Foelkersam. On all sides, whistles were shrilling and officers were bellowing orders. The alarm had been raised. A bare-headed Hungarian colonel rushed at them, pistol in hand. Von Foelkersam knocked it from his grasp and they ran on. Another Hungarian came into view. Skorzeny grabbed him.

'Lead us to the Commandant of the Burgberg – at once!' he commanded.

The Hungarian obeyed. Tamely he ran on with the assault group, giving them instructions. Now deep inside the fortress, they could hear the muted snap-and-crackle of a fire fight coming from outside. Still no one attempted to bar their excited progress.

Skorzeny rushed into a room. A Hungarian was crouched behind a machine gun at the window. Sergeant Holzer, pushed by Skorzeny, grabbed the weapon and flung it out of the window to the courtyard below. The Hungarian surrendered. Skorzeny pushed on. Another door loomed up and, surprisingly enough, Skorzeny, panting, stopped and knocked on it. It was opened by a Hungarian major-general and the SS giant knew he had found his man.

'Are you the Commandant of the Burgberg?' he snapped and then without waiting for the general to answer, he cried, 'I demand you surrender the Burgberg at once! You are responsible if any more blood is spilled. I ask you for an immediate decision!'

Tamely the general gave in. 'I surrender the Burgberg to you and will order immediate cessation of hostilities,' he said.

The two men shook hands and it was all over. Horthy was in Skorzeny's hands.

At the cost of twenty German casualties, Admiral Horthy had been captured, to be sent to Germany by special train 'as a guest of the Leader' and replaced immediately by the pro-German Count Szalasi. The latter ordered the Hungarian army to take up arms against the Russians at once, so that the Hungarians fought loyally at Germany's side when all its other allies had long deserted it. After nearly a year of failures, Otto Skorzeny had pulled off a tremendous coup. Now he relaxed in the captured fortification, living like 'the king in France', as the German expression has it, drinking choice Tokay, eating fine foods, even bathing in the baroque tub used by his former Emperor, Franz-Josef of Austria. But the time out of war was not going to last very long. Things were moving in the West, and Adolf Hitler, who had ordered this reward for the man who had 'saved the German Central Front' in the East, would need the scar-faced giant again soon.

2

On the afternoon of 21 October 1944, Skorzeny was ordered to report to the Führer's main HQ at the 'Wolf's Lair'.* Already the Russians were only a few hours away from the HQ. But that fact didn't seem to worry Hitler. Pale and shaken as he was from the July attempt on his life and the sixty-odd tablets and pills he took each day, Hitler received Skorzeny with enthusiasm. Taking the giant's hand in both his in the Austrian fashion, he told Skorzeny, '*Das haben Sie gut gemacht, lieber Skorzeny,*' and added that he had promoted Skorzeny to the rank of lieutenant-colonel in the SS and awarded him the German Cross in Gold, known commonly

---

* In his early days, Hitler had often used the cover-name of 'Wolf'; hence the name of his HQ.

among German private soldiers as the 'Order of the Scrambled Egg', on account of its shape and colour.

Then Hitler, still holding the giant's hand, led him to the *Sitzecke*, the 'sitting-corner', common to all German offices, where, after he had taken his seat, he asked Skorzeny to do the same and tell him all about Operations 'Mickey Mouse' and 'Bazooka'. Obediently Skorzeny did so while Hitler listened attentively, occasionally laughing out loud at some of Skorzeny's outrageous remarks. Finally Skorzeny was finished and rose to depart, but Hitler detained him.

'Stay awhile,' he commanded, new resolution in his pale, worn face, 'I have something to tell you.'

Skorzeny sat down again.

For a moment or two, Hitler remained silent, as if, somehow, he were in doubt if he really should disclose what was going on in his mind at this moment. Abruptly then, he began. 'Skorzeny,' he said, his voice excited, 'I am now going to give you the most important job of your life. Up to now only very few people know of my preparations and secret plan in which you will play a great role.'

He paused and Skorzeny waited tensely.

Hitler's eyes sparkled, 'Skorzeny, in December, Germany will commence a great offensive which will be decisive for the future of our country!'

Skorzeny's face must have revealed his shock, surprise, doubt; for Hitler hurried on with, 'The world thinks Germany is finished, with only the day and hour of the funeral to be appointed. I am going to show how mistaken they are. The corpse will rise and hurl itself in fury at the West. Then we shall see.'

Now for the next hour, while Skorzeny listened awe-struck, Hitler explained that while Germany fought for its life on the Western frontier, with the Allies pressing into the Reich from Holland to northern France, he had considered just where to strike back.

Five main operations had come in for detailed examination: a counter-attack into Holland at Venlo; two into central Luxembourg; one at Metz; and finally, an attack into Alsace. All the pros and cons had been discussed in detail and certain firm conclusions about where the great attack would go in had been reached. Later Colonel-General Jodl, Hitler's Chief-of-Staff, would explain them to Skorzeny.

Now, however, Hitler said, 'I have told you so much so that you will realise that everything has been considered very carefully and has been well worked out. . . . Now you and your units will play a very important part in this offensive. As an advance guard you will capture one or more bridges on the River Meuse between Liège and Namur.' Hitler paused for a moment before saying slowly, 'You will carry out this operation in British or American uniform!'

Skorzeny does not record in his own account of that memorable meeting his reaction to Hitler's news, save that he was 'confused'. Perhaps, however, his face revealed his shock that he and his men would be going into action dressed in enemy uniform, which meant that if they were captured they could be shot as spies; for Hitler said swiftly, 'The enemy has already used this trick. Only a couple of days ago I received news that the Americans dressed in German uniforms during their operations in Aachen. Now in addition to capturing the bridges, you will send out small commando parties in enemy uniform to destroy communications, give false orders, change sign-posts, etc., etc., and generally create confusion in the Allied ranks. And all your preparations have to be completed by the first of December.'

Skorzeny tried to protest that the time would be too short. But as always Hitler never listened when he was set on an idea. 'I know you will do your best.'

Numbly Skorzeny rose to go and meet Jodl for further details. Hitler went with him to the door. There he paused before the two of them went into the operations room, where the cunning-faced little staff officer was waiting for them with his maps: 'But now to the most important thing, Skorzeny.' He looked up at the giant, his face suddenly hard and determined. *'Total, absolute secrecy!'*

Skorzeny nodded, his mind racing.

'Only a very few people know about the offensive, Skorzeny,' Hitler continued. 'In order to conceal your preparations from your troops, stick to this basic cover-plan which we have worked out. Tell them that we are expecting a full-scale enemy attack in the area between Cologne and

Bonn. Your preparations are intended to be part of the resistance to that attack.'

The great deception in the West, which would lead to what has been called the 'European Pearl Harbor' had commenced.

3

One year before, in the spring of 1943 when Otto Skorzeny had first hit the headlines with his dramatic rescue of the Duce from his mountain fastness, an ex-sailor of the Dutch Royal Navy was preparing to return to his homeland after two long years of exile. Together with two companions, 25-year-old Pieter Dourlein, recruited into the British SOE* by a certain Major Anthony Blunt, 'a small and jovial Englishman', who one day would turn out to be a traitor, was now flying over the coast of occupied Holland, ready to parachute into the night.

Now it was 01.15 hours on the morning of 10 March 1943, and the big RAF Halifax bomber was steadily approaching the dropping zone beyond the small town of Apeldoorn. Suddenly there was fleck of crimson light below, the signal beacon. It was the DZ. The pilot came lower. The three Dutch SOE men who were soon going to parachute themselves into the unknown positioned themselves tensely at the door. An icy wind whipped their coveralls about their young bodies. But there was no turning back now. The jump-master gave his orders, hard and brisk. *One . . . two . . . three!* They went out in a great hurry, the wind clutching them with greedy fingers. For a novice, the ex-sailor didn't make a bad landing. He got stuck in the leafless branches of a tree, but escaped with just a few scratches. Hastily he released himself and dropped into the undergrowth, pistol at the ready.

Slowly the drone of the Halifax's engines died away as the plane headed back to England and the crew's breakfast of

---

* Special Operations Executive, a secret service organization, equivalent to the US Office of Strategic Services (OSS), forerunner of the CIA.

bacon and eggs, the usual reward for a hazardous mission. Now there was total silence. Not a sound, neither Dutch nor German voices. Dourlein might have been the last man on earth.

Suddenly there was a sound. Heavy boots walking through the grass. Germans? Dourlein clutched the pistol more firmly in a sweat-damp hand. If they were the Moppen,* they wouldn't take him alive! A first cautious black figure came into view. He prepared to fire. Suddenly someone called his code-name softly: 'Paul . . . Paul. . . .' Dourlein stifled a sigh of relief. It was the reception committee!

Hands were shaken, backs were slapped. Dourlein handed the two men who had come to welcome him a small flask of whisky with which each agent was equipped before being dropped, and they toasted one another before setting off on the journey to join the main party, who had already found his two comrades.

By now it was four o'clock in the morning. A tired but happy Dourlein was looking forward to getting under cover at last and sleeping. Suddenly he was very tired. Tramping through the frosty grass, Dourlein let his head hang so that he did not notice the glance his two companions exchanged. It was unfortunate for him. Abruptly the two of them rushed him. His arms were twisted behind his back. He heard the click of handcuffs. For a moment Dourlein could not make out what had happened. 'Don't start larking about now,' he protested wearily, thinking they were playing a game on him.

But this was no game. A pistol was thrust roughly into his back. A whistle shrilled. Men were coming out of the bushes on all sides and a cynical voice was saying in perfect Dutch: 'Well, well, so you thought you'd be clever and jump from an English plane, did you? . . . You've been caught by the German counter-espionage. . . . You've been betrayed and we've got the whole of your organisation in our hands.'

He was led away, head bowed in defeat, captured even before he could start his mission. Yet another spy had gone into Major Giskes' trap, and another little whisky flask would

---

* Dutch name for the Germans, equivalent of 'kraut'

decorate the German major's mantelpiece as a souvenir. Before he was finished there would be forty-odd of them up there, each signifying another dead spy.

Major Hermann Giskes, middle-aged, sardonic and clever, had joined the German Abwehr just before the war on the advice of a friend who told him he'd be shot to pieces if he went back to the Regular Army once Hitler started his war. Almost immediately the ex-travelling salesman from the Rhineland was involved in counter-espionage against the British, helping to break up the 'Z-Ring', the major SIS* operation on the Continent. Thereafter followed spy-catching operations in the Low Countries and France until finally Giskes, now a Major, was posted in November 1941 to Holland. In a mere two years he had passed from an apprentice, who had known absolutely nothing about the clandestine world of intelligence, to a master, with all the dirty tricks of his trade – bribery, corruption, blackmail and worse – at his fingertips. Now he was to become the greatest spy catcher of them all.

In the same month that Giskes took up his Dutch appointment, a fat, lame Dutchman named Gregg Ridderhof, a small-time crook, who spoke an odd mixture of Dutch, English and Spanish when he was drunk, which was often, volunteered to work for Giskes. The latter accepted the offer though he disliked Ridderhof intensely.

A short time later Ridderhof sent in a written report, stating that British intelligence had parachuted two Dutch agents into the country, Hubertus Lauwers and Thijs Taconis, to set up a spy ring in Holland. The thin-lipped major, with his rosy cheeks and perennially sardonic smile on his face, read the report, and then wrote in the margin, somewhat angrily, '*Gehen Sie zum Nordpol mit Ihren Geschichten.*' ('Go to the North Pole with your tales'). Giskes knew his Dutch traitors. They'd tell any kind of wild tale for money. Giskes' comment irritated the fat crook. His professional honour was hurt. In the next two months he worked hard to prove that Radio Orange, the Free Dutch Radio

---

* The British Secret Intelligence Service

station in London, was being used to announce the dropping zones for the landing of their agents in Holland.

Now Giskes was convinced, especially when on 1 March 1942, as Ridderhof had predicted, an RAF bomber dropped weapons to a Dutch resistance group headed by 'Long Thijs', a tall man whose real name was Taconis, a member of the Dutch branch of the SOE, working under the command of Major Blunt and Captain Bingham.

Giskes had a stroke of genius that March day in the middle of the war, seated in that discreet brown-stone villa which was his HQ. Instead of arresting the whole bunch of them, he'd take them prisoner – and make them work for *him*! Operation 'North Pole' (the reference was to his first angry comment on Ridderhof's report) was born.

By the summer of 1942, the captured Dutch agents forced to work for the Germans had thirty DZs in operation, working together with the British. Giskes even sent Luftwaffe planes into the sky to search for suitable 'secret' sites for the unsuspecting RAF! Agent after agent came floating down, straight into the waiting Germans' arms.

At first Giskes would turn out to receive them personally, allowing them to take a drink out of that little whisky flask, before having the startled, confused agent whisked off to the converted seminary of Haaren, which was his secret prison. Later there were so many of them that he became bored with the whole business. He was getting 'too old for those cold night waits', he told himself, and left the business of 'welcoming' the para-agents to his subordinates. But he did insist on being given each new agent's whisky flask as a 'souvenir'.*

Operation 'North Pole' was an unqualified success. Nearly fifty agents went into the bag, and the booty was tremendous. For the first time the Germans were able to obtain the new British secret weapon – plastic explosive. Valuable foreign currency, dollars, pounds, even gold, came floating down like

---

* In the old folks' home where he passed his last years, these macabre souvenirs held pride of place, but when the author visited him there they had been carefully moved.

manna from heaven. Nearly 12,000 hand weapons were secured, and at least twelve British and American four-engined bombers were shot down during the course of the drops.

Berlin was impressed. Even the SS could not conceal their admiration, though the chiefs of the SS secret service hated their rivals of the army's Abwehr with a passion. They sent the new head of their SS Hunting Commando (SS Jagdkommando), a hulking giant just invalided out of the Adolf Hitler Bodyguard Division, one Otto Skorzeny, to study Giskes' methods.

Skorzeny was astonished by what he found taking place in Holland, and recorded later that he 'followed the operation with the greatest of interest'. To try Giskes out, he 'ordered' a new, one-shot, silenced British revolver from London. Four-teen days later it was 'delivered' from London, courtesy of the RAF.

Skorzeny tried it out there and then. Opening the window of Giskes' office, he took aim at one of the ducks serenely sailing along the canal outside. He pulled the trigger. There was a soft plop. The duck keeled over, dead. None of the Dutch civilians promenading along on the paths on either side of the canal took the slightest notice.

Skorzeny was suitably impressed, and went back to his chiefs in Berlin to report very favourably on Major Hermann Giskes and his operation. Giskes, who would not meet Skorzeny again till long after the war when both had become famous – or perhaps more accurately infamous – was not so taken with the giant with whom, unwittingly, he would associate in the last great German intelligence operation of the war. 'Big, bold, brave', was Giskes' post-war verdict, 'but not all too bright!'

On the night of Sunday, 29 August 1943, Pieter Dourlein, a prisoner at Haaren Seminary these six months now, set about bringing Giskes' cunning, cruel 'England game' (*England-spiel*) to an end. He decided to escape. On Sunc ' morning Dourlein rose early. His two cellmates pleaded wiṭṭ him not to go. 'For God's sake', one of them, van der Boor, said tearfully, 'Pieter, don't go. They'll only shoot you!'

But Dourlein was not to be deflected. He started to make his preparations. Supper came, a pail of soup thrust through the cell door. As soon as the guard who had brought it had gone, Pieter stripped and knocked on the wall of the cell. Next door Johann Ubbink, who was to escape with him, answered. It was the signal to go.

'I sprang on the bed,' Dourlein recalled after the war, 'pulled the nail out which held up the window and looked down the corridor. Everything clear! A bit further ahead I saw a blond head looking out too. A few moments later my future companion' (Dourlein had never seen Ubbink up to now) 'and I were both in the corridor. Our pals reached us our clothes and the rope. Together we ran into an empty cell which we knew was never locked. We looked at each other for the first time and slapped each other on the back.'

But there was no time to be wasted on congratulations. The two escapees slipped into their clothes, and waited anxiously as the heavy tread of a guard passed, then crept in stocking-feet to the latrine. It was empty.

They slipped inside and locked the door. Here they planned to wait for hours until the prison had settled down for the night before continuing their escape. Twice in the long, leaden hours of their wait, guards rattled the door, and each time one of them cried with feigned anger, '*Besetzt, Mensch!*' ('Occupied, man!').

At last they decided it was time to go. They forced the latrine window and squeezed through its bars; by now both of them were terribly thin. The icy cold light of the searchlight swept by. They started paying out their rope to the ground, 36 feet below. Pieter went down first, followed by Johann. Just in time. The searchlight swept by an instant later.

Now the two young men were out of the prison. But there were other obstacles to be overcome. 'Now', Pieter recalled, 'we had to get over the barbed wire fences about 55 yards away. We approached them carefully. Suddenly we heard steps – the sound of heavily nailed boots. A guard! But the man didn't notice us and carried on.'

Wiping away the sweat on their brows in spite of the coolness of the summer night, the two Dutchmen crawled closer to the last big obstacle. Johann pulled himself upright and took a deep breath. He launched himself forward for a high jump and cleared the fence with inches to spare. Now it was Pieter's turn. He prayed fervently he'd make it. He hurtled forward and cleared it too.

'We were free!' he wrote later, reliving that wonderful moment. 'Beside ourselves with joy, we fell into each other's arms. But we knew that the end was not yet in sight.'

They had a long odyssey through occupied Europe before they finally reached England, where they were imprisoned because the Dutchmen operating under Giskes' command had radioed London immediately, after the two of them had escaped, that Dourlein and Ubbink were German agents. It was not until the early summer of 1944 that the British authorities believed them. Hermann Giskes, the supreme realist, knew immediately that the game was up, however. Later he wrote, 'It was clear to me that the bottom had been knocked out of the whole *Englandspiel*.' But his sardonic humour did not desert him in spite of his disappointment. He had his Dutch operators send one final message to the SOE HQ in Baker Street, London. It read:

> To Messrs Blunt, Bingham and Successors, Ltd, stop. You are trying to do business in the Netherlands without our assistance, stop. We think this rather unfair in view of our long and successful co-operation as your sole agent, stop. But never mind, whenever you pay a visit to the Continent you may rest assured that you will be received with the same care as all those you sent us before, stop. So long.

The reaction of the first-mentioned addressee, who was already working as a double agent himself (for the Russians), the future Sir Anthony Blunt, Keeper of the Queen's Pictures, has not been recorded. Perhaps it was amusement in view of his own devious game.

4

However, the promised reception did not occur. The Allies invaded and swept all before them. Giskes, too, was swept up with the fleeing German army. For a while he hung on in Brussels, again infiltrating agents behind the Allied lines, including the notorious 'King Kong', suspected by some of betraying the Arnhem landing. From there he also directed his Austrian agent 'Freddie', who, married to Jean de Broglie, a member of French high society, now reported from American-occupied Paris. (Aristocratic Jean de Broglie was no ordinary member of that 1944 jet set. A scion of the Singer sewing-machine family, she was related to no less a person than Winston Churchill himself!)

Late in the summer of 1944 Jean went to London on the invitation of her second cousin (she had been engaged in some minor resistance work during the German occupation), and Freddie followed her two months later in the uniform of a captain in the British army. 'He volunteered,' Giskes explained after the war. 'He wasn't blackmailed into doing so. He even worked out his own means of communicating with me.' In November 1944, however, Freddie disappeared, and Giskes' hopes of infiltrating an agent right into the Churchill family itself were dashed.* After nearly five years of counter-espionage and running spy rings, Giskes, now a Lieutenant-Colonel, found himself washed up on Germany's south-west frontier, his old Abwehr friends either killed by the enemy or by Hitler's minions as traitors, with not a single agent in place. Giskes realised he was almost out of a job.

In early November, however, Lieutenant-Colonel Giskes received a summons to attend the headquarters of Field Marshal Model, commanding German Army Group 'B', whose job was to defend the Reich's long frontier with the Low Countries and northern France. No details of the summons were given, and Giskes motored through the autumnal forests of the Eifel from his own modest HQ just outside Bonn in a mood of pent-up excitement; after all, it was not every day that a field marshal invited a lowly colonel of intelligence to attend him, especially when the former chief of that intelligence service, Admiral Canaris, was currently in a

---

* According to Giskes' statement to the author, Freddie survived, was forced to divorce Jean to obtain his freedom and is still alive in Austria.

concentration camp on a charge of high treason. In the autumn of 1944 senior German generals wanted nothing to do with supposed traitors, and those who had associated with them. You were likely to end up hanging by the jaw from a butcher's hook like an animal carcass if you did, or being garrotted slowly to death by chicken wire.*

Model received Giskes and another colonel of intelligence just before lunch at his headquarters at a secluded forester's lodge just outside the idyllic Eifel tourist town of Münstereifel. Model was a small man, monocled, with somewhat bulging eyes, aggressive, feared by his commanders and beloved by his soldiers. As usual, he did not waste time. Without taking his eyes off the two colonels, he barked, 'Can you think of any plan which would fool the Western Allies as to the strategic intentions of my Army Command? And, by the way, it must involve Allied nationals so that it would be entirely convincing?'

Giskes' companion answered straight away that it would be impossible. At this stage of the war it was almost ninety-nine per cent certain that no Allied national in his right mind would want to work for the Germans.

Giskes wasn't so certain. Old fox that he was, he took his time. He knew that both his own organisation and Skorzeny's SS Jagdkommando had established so-called 'sleeper organisations', composed of French, Belgian, Dutch and Luxembourg nationals, before the German army had fled from those countries. For all he knew, such people might still work for Germany when the call came. He told Model, therefore, that he needed exactly four hours to think about it. Model agreed and strode away, leaving Giskes with the Chief-of-Intelligence of Army Group 'B'.

The latter gave Giskes an excellent lunch and then left him alone to think about the problem. It was a typical November day in the Eifel, dark, with grey wisps of fog curling around the fir trees outside. From far away came the muted noise of the heavy artillery firing in the battle of Hürtgen Forest, where the German infantry held on desperately

---

*The fate of several of the generals who had taken part in the army plot against the Führer in July 1944.

against the overwhelming weight of the American attack. Giskes might have thought that all new plans were purposeless; Germany had already lost the war. Why bother? Or perhaps, after five years at the 'great game', as the British called it, he might have been bitten by the bug – might not have been able to escape the heady atmosphere of the war-in-the-shadows. We do not know. But on that afternoon in that remote forester's lodge, with the fog trickling out of the woods, he made his decision.

At three o'clock precisely he saw the Chief-of-Intelligence again. First he made a request; he asked if he could be informed of Army Group 'B's' strategic plans. By now he had guessed that a counter-offensive in the West was behind Model's summons.

The Chief-of-Intelligence was quite adamant. No, he could not disclose Model's objective or plans. Giskes had to take his word for it that a great new operation in the West was already well beyond the planning stage and would shake the 'Anglo-American bandits' out of their self-satisfied complacency. Giskes accepted the condition. 'All right, sir,' he replied, 'I shall get to work on it immediately.' He hesitated a moment and smiled, 'But what if, in preparing a fake cover-plan to feed to the enemy, by mistake . . . I hit on the real offensive?'

Model's Chief-of-Intelligence was not amused.

5

Oberst der Fallschirmtruppe* Baron von der Heydte came late to the great clandestine operation being planned in the West; and it was clear from the very start that he didn't like it, for his was a cool, collected mind, not given to the wild, daring schemes of a Skorzeny or the ruthless cunning of a Hermann Giskes. After ten years of soldiering von der Heydte could not forget that he was an aristocrat belonging to what the

---

* Colonel of parachute troops

Germans call the '*Altadel*'* and a trained academic jurist. Indeed, within half a decade of his being summoned to take his part in the new operation, he would be a professor of international law.

Baron von der Heydte came of a long line of Bavarian Catholics and was related to most of the great families of Europe. With his strange, long, almost ascetic face and pronounced front teeth, he would have looked just as much at home wearing a crusader's helmet as he did wearing the rimless one of the German paras. In 1933, aged 26, he was the assistant to the Professor of Law at the University of Berlin. Unfortunately, the Professor was both a Jew and a social democrat, not a winning combination in the year that Hitler came to power. Inevitably, the Professor lost his job. As was customary, von der Heydte left too, took up a Carnegie Foundation Scholarship and studied for the next two years in Vienna, Paris and Italy. In 1935 he returned to Germany and won a commission in the Wehrmacht's 15th Cavalry Regiment, stationed in arch-conservative and Catholic Paderborn. There, for the last years of the peace, von der Heydte went into what the Germans called 'inner emigration' against the Nazis, according to his own statements, although he had been a member of the SA student movement and von Papen's right-wing Catholic movement.

Von der Heydte's first two years of war were uneventful, and it was 1941 before he saw any real action. On 20 May of that year he commanded one of the attack battalions of the 3rd Parachute Regiment in the German invasion of Crete. He landed separated from the rest of his men, as was common in parachute operations. He was trying to find his way through the bakingly hot Cretan fields, heading for the sound of the firing, when suddenly came the screech of engines, followed by the fierce crackle of machine guns: 'I hurled myself into the ditch automatically . . . and at that moment a German fighter with all guns blazing swept over within a few feet of where I

---

* 'Old aristocracy', to distinguish it from the new aristocracy created by the Hohenzollerns between 1871 and 1918.

lay. . . . So the first shots aimed at me during the attack had been fired by one of my fellow countrymen!'

But von der Heydte survived to win the Knight's Cross for his capture of the village of Canea. Thereafter he fought in Italy, and by the spring of 1944 he was commanding the élite 6th Parachute Regiment in Normandy. During the months before the great invasion, von der Heydte's regiment was visited by Field Marshal Rommel himself.

After dinner in the mess, Rommel took von der Heydte to one side, and said, 'Heydte, are you sure of your regiment?'

'Absolutely, *Herr Feldmarschall*,' said von der Heydte, half-guessing what Rommel meant.

'You are sure of every man?' Rommel persisted.

'Completely.'

'If need be, they would obey you alone?' Rommel barked, making his meaning now quite clear; for von der Heydte, whose cousin was Colonel Claus von Stauffenberg, the officer who would place the bomb in an attempt to assassinate Hitler on 20 July, knew that the army wanted peace with the Western Allies before it was too late. And the only way they were going to achieve that aim was by getting rid of Hitler.

'Me alone,' von der Heydte replied adamantly.

'We want a lot of units like yours,' the Field Marshal, who soon would be forced to commit suicide for his part in the 20 July plot, concluded.

Nothing came of the plot, but all the same Colonel von der Heydte was not boasting. He had turned his 6th Parachute Regiment into a sort of personal legion, taking only volunteers wherever possible, bound to him by a special kind of loyalty. All new recruits to his regiment were received by the Colonel personally, who told them: 'From the moment a man volunteers for the airborne troops and joins my regiment, he enters a new order of humanity. He is ruled by one law only, that of our unit. He must give up personal weaknesses and ambitions and realise that our battle is for the existence of the whole German nation.'

All von der Heydte's men had to learn his 'ten commandments' too, which began with Commandment Number One: *'You are the élite of the German Army. You are to seek out combat and to be ready to endure hardship. Your greatest ambition should be to do battle'*; and ended with Commandment Number Ten: *'Never surrender. For you it is either victory or death; there is no other alternative. This is a point of honour.'*

In the battle of Normandy von der Heydte's paratroopers proved just how well they had learned those ten commandments. They were in action right from the start against the American paratroopers of the US 101st Airborne Division, the 'Screaming Eagles'. Indeed, his men drove almost to Utah Beach but were stopped by the 'Screaming Eagles'' stubborn defence of the first French township to be captured in the great invasion, Ste-Mère Eglise.

By the middle of July 1944, after seven weeks of solid combat, von der Heydte pulled back what was left of the regiment through a full armoured regiment of the US First Army, leading them 'like a Red Indian chief', as his commander General Student reported proudly to the author.

Most of them were sick or wounded and had to be sent down 'hospital alley', as the paras called the road to the military hospital at Alençon. A mere sixty men were left on their feet unwounded. More than 3,000 officers and men had been killed in action or were missing.

In the first week of December 1944, Colonel von der Heydte, now commander of the parachute army's parachute school at Bergen Op Zoom in Holland, received an urgent summons to report to the HQ of General Student, who had conquered Holland in 1940 and Crete in 1941 with his beloved paras.

Student was in a good mood. In World War I he had fought as a fighter pilot, but had been regarded as too old to make a parachute jump when he had been given command of the first German parachute division. Because he had never jumped into combat he was nicknamed 'Father Student' by his subordinates, who had sprung into space for him over Europe and Russia. Recently, however, after years of command jobs, he had been engaged in active operations against the Anglo-American paras dropped in September in Montgomery's abortive 'Market Garden' Operation,* and the excitement seemed to have taken years off him.

Eagerly he now received von der Heydte. For after two years without any large-scale parachute operations, his paras were going into action again – out of the sky instead of marching into battle like ordinary 'stubble-hoppers'.†

Swiftly Student outlined the plan. The Führer, he told von der Heydte, had decided to undertake a major offensive in which a parachute detachment would be employed. Von der Heydte was to form and command this force.

The Colonel learned that he was expected to jump behind the Soviet troops surrounding the German bridgehead on the River Vistula in Poland. It seemed logical to him that the High Command was preparing a surprise offensive to relieve this sector of the Eastern Front, which was under heavy pressure by the Red army.

Then Student passed on to the composition of the force to be under von der Heydte's command. For security reasons the Baron was not to take men either from the Bergen Op Zoom jump school or his own old regiment. Instead, each of the four divisions under Student's command would contribute men, though he would select his own staff and company commanders. Von der Heydte didn't like the idea much. He knew the army too well. Divisional commanders might well recommend to their subordinate commanders to send von der Heydte the best men available. In the event, however, he'd get the misfits, the men the subordinate commanders didn't want. It had always been thus, in every army in the world. All the same, he didn't object , for he had to admit he was excited at the thought of leading men into action again from the air for the first time since Crete in May 1941, a time which now seemed to belong to another world.

'In a few days' time', Student continued, 'I shall send you 1,200 experienced paras to the collecting point at Aalten [Holland]. I'll leave it to you how you structure your battle group, von der Heydte.' Student leaned forward significantly, and said, 'But you must have the men organised by 13

---

* The great airborne landing in Holland
† Contemptuous German army name for infantry

December. Von der Heydte, with effect from 5.30 on the morning of the fourteenth *you must be ready for action!'* Thus for the first time one of the three colonels learned the date for the start of an offensive against the Western Allies.*

---

* In fact, of course, it commenced at 05.30 hours on 16 December

TWO

The Ghost Front

1

In the winter of 1944, Allied intelligence seemed to be asleep. By mid-September, the Western Allies had felt imminent victory in their hands. Flushed with their great victories of the summer, the enemy having fled behind his own borders and the Reich tottering to its knees, the Anglo-American intelligence chiefs shared the confident opinion of the fighting commanders that it could be a matter of only weeks, perhaps even days, before the 'thousand-year Reich' collapsed.

The bitter fighting of late autumn at Aachen, in Hürtgen Forest and northern France disillusioned them a little, but the old optimism of September never finally vanished. Indeed, when the Allied armies began to attack again in late November and early December, the early optimism flared up again. Four days before the US Twelfth Army Group's front disintegrated, General Sibert, Bradley's* Chief-of-Intelligence, issued an intelligence summary, stating that 'it is now certain that attrition is steadily sapping the strength of German forces on the Western front and that the crust of defenses is thinner, more brittle and more vulnerable than it appears on our G–2 maps or to the troops in the line'. And it was an optimism that was shared by most of the Allied intelligence chiefs.

Further to the rear, intelligence chiefs had virtually forgotten about the German army. To them it appeared that

---

* General Omar Bradley, commander of the Army Group

continued German resistance depended wholly upon Hitler. Eliminate the Führer, and what was left of the Reich would collapse like a house of cards.

That winter there were protracted discussions at the highest level in Washington to consider how to assassinate Hitler. When, for instance, General Donovan, the burly, tough ex-lawyer who was head of the OSS, learned that Hitler was to meet his fellow-dictator Mussolini at the Brenner Pass, he asked for suggestions on what might be done. A representative of the organisation's SO (subversive operations) snorted, 'Let us parachute a cadre of our toughest men into the area and shoot up the bastards! Sure, it'll be a suicide operation, but that's what we're organised to carry out.'

Donovan smiled and turned to his scientific adviser, Dr Stanley P. Lovell, a middle-aged scientist in charge of the OSS's 'Department of Dirty Tricks'.* Donovan called him 'Professor Moriarty' after the villain of the Sherlock Holmes stories. 'How would Professor Moriarty capitalize on this situation?' he asked.

Lovell, as always, was ready with a novel and lethal scheme. 'I propose an attack which they cannot anticipate. They'll meet in the conference room of an inn or a hotel. If we can have one operator for five minutes or less in that room just before they gather there, that is really all we need.'

Lovell's colleagues looked sceptical, but Lovell went on to explain: 'I suggest that he brings in a vase filled with cut flowers in water and that he places it on the conference table or nearby. In his hand will be a capsule containing liquid nitrogen–mustard gas. It's a new chemical derivative which has no odour whatever, is colourless and floats on water. I have it available in my laboratory.' Lovell let his listeners absorb the information before continuing. 'As our man places the bouquet on the conference table, he crushes the capsule and drops it among the flowers. An invisible oily film spreads over the water in the dish and starts vaporising. Our man gets

---

*It is interesting to note that forty years ago the forerunner of the CIA had already established most of those departments and techniques which have gained so much notoriety in recent years.

out safely, and I think he should disappear into Switzerland if possible.'

'Professor Moriarty's' suggestion was one that Conan Doyle himself could not have improved upon, and General Donovan was suitably impressed. 'What happens to the men at the conference?' he asked.

Lovell explained. 'Well, if they are in the room for twenty minutes, the invisible gas will affect their bodies through their eyeballs. Everyone in that room will be permanently blinded. The optic nerve will be atrophied. A blind leader can't continue the war – at least, I don't believe he can.'

As Lovell had anticipated, his macabre suggestion aroused excited interest and controversy among the OSS men assembled in Donovan's office, but 'Professor Moriarty' hadn't finished yet. 'There's a big pay-off possible, if it is done. Let's be bold in capitalising on the event. The Pope might be persuaded to pronounce this blindness to be a warning that the Axis powers should lay down their arms and return to the ways of peace, having flouted the sixth commandment, "Thou shalt not kill".'

Dr Lovell turned to Donovan, who was a strict Catholic, and said, 'General, a great number of the German fighting forces – and the Italian too – are Roman Catholics. They will heed Pius XII. If he can use his high office to stop this killing, isn't he advancing the cause of Christianity more than any man on earth?'

Although Donovan promised to discuss the matter with Cardinal Spellman, nothing came of the scheme, for Hitler survived his meeting with Mussolini that year. Undismayed, 'Professor Moriarty' tried again. Working on the basis of the top secret psychological study of Hitler made by a Dr Lange (which was to remain classified for another thirty years) Lovell came to the conclusion that Hitler's' poor emotional control, his violent passions, his selection of companions like Roehm* 'indicated that the Führer was on the borderline between male and female'. Lovell felt it might be possible to nudge him to the female side in the hope that 'his moustache would fall off and his voice become soprano'.

---

* A well-known homosexual

His plan involved smuggling a gardener into his entourage who would doctor the home-grown vegetables for his personal table with female sex hormones. These would upset Hitler's whole hormonal balance and radically affect his direction of the war.

It is not surprising in that crazy Washington of the winter of 1944, where the OSS was the joke of the cocktail circuit ('Oh, So Silly' and 'Organisation Shush-Shush' were among mocking interpretations of its initials), that the scheme was approved, but Lovell heard no more of it. As he wrote later in his account of his schemes in the 'Department of Dirty Tricks', *Of Spies and Stratagems*, 'Since Hitler survived, I can only assume that the gardener took our money and threw the syringes and medications into the nearest thicket. Either that or Hitler had a big turnover in "tasters".'

While the three colonels worked feverishly on their own schemes to catch the Americans by surprise on the Western Front, the OSS in Washington did not have a monopoly on crazy plans and weird and wonderful schemes for clandestine operations in the Reich, of which they now knew so little. In London, too, the SOE, the OSS's rival and one-time teacher, was also dreaming up some hare-brained ideas for secret missions.

Inspired, ironically enough, by Skorzeny's daring rescue of Mussolini from the Gran Sasso in September 1943, the heads of the SOE began toying with the idea of a bold raid on Hitler's HQ. All September 1944, the scheme was under serious discussion, but then suddenly, with no reason given, it was dropped, only to be replaced by another plan.

Six years before, Colonel MacFarlane, a former intelligence officer and then military attaché in the British Embassy in Berlin, had worked out a plan to assassinate Hitler. Armed with a silenced telescopic rifle, he would shoot Hitler from the balcony of his flat in the Charlottenburg Chaussee. He put the plan forward to Chamberlain's Government, but they turned it down as unsportsmanlike.

By the winter of 1944, the British powers-that-be no longer paid heed to such considerations. Under General Templar,

newly posted to command the SOE's German Section, a
scheme was put forward to kill Hitler outright.

Captured German generals imprisoned in the UK were
quizzed about what they knew of his headquarters. Information was also obtained about Hitler's security arrangements
and the personnel of his *Führerbegleitkommando*, his personal
bodyguards. Detailed sketches of his private court – Morrell,
his doctor, and Linge, his butler, among them – were drawn
up. For the first time information was supplied by captured
German senior officers about his secret mistress, Eva Braun.

Again, in the end nothing came of this plan, and Templar
decided to discontinue the attempt to kill Hitler. He argued
that it would be a waste of British lives now that Hitler's Reich
was about to tumble down. All the Allies had to do was to wait
– until Hitler's armies, lacking men, planes, tanks, fuel,
ammunition – and spirit – gave up; until the day when their
Führer threw in the sponge and blew out his brains. Besides,
the intelligence bosses in London and Washington, as well as
their senior colleagues with the armies fighting on the Continent, reasoned that if – and it was a big if – anything untoward
were to happen, the 'Boffins of Bletchley' would warn them
well in advance. They had done so for years now. Why should
there be any change in this last winter of the war?

Closer to the front, the more junior intelligence men were not
quite so optimistic as their superiors. The German army was
not finished yet by a long chalk. After all, the US army was
evacuating approximately 7,000 battle casualties each day. In
the opinion of these junior intelligence men, the German
soldier would resist as long as he was told to, especially now
that he was fighting on his own soil.

All agreed, however, that the future role of the German
army would be strictly defensive. The return of Field Marshal
Gerd von Rundstedt to the Supreme Command of the German forces in the West in late September had convinced these
intelligence men that the German soldier would fight a conventional battle. He would act and react according to the
rational and accepted principles of military science. Knowing
von Rundstedt's strategy from the past, they assumed that he
would husband his resources, falling back only when forced

to, launching medium-sized counter-attacks for strategic purposes (say, in the Aachen–Düren region), until he reached the Rhine. Here, at Germany's last natural barrier, he would stand and make his last fight.

What they didn't know was that the aged Field Marshal, given now to a little too much cognac and sleeping late, was merely a figurehead. 'The little Bohemian corporal', as he called Hitler contemptuously behind his back, wielded the real power; all the authority he possessed, as he complained bitterly to his cronies, was that 'to change the sentry outside my door'.

But even the most optimistic of these young junior intelligence officers, who believed they knew exactly how Germany would fight its last battles before the final collapse, were worried by one thing. Germany had lost an army, indeed its most powerful army, one favoured by Hitler with the best equipment and the best available men because it was the only SS army in the whole of the Wehrmacht.

After the débâcle of France and the fighting withdrawal into the Low Countries and over the frontier into Germany proper, all the armoured divisions of what was to become the Sixth SS Panzer Army, commanded by the former Nazi Party bully-boy, Bavarian Sepp Dietrich, had been withdrawn for refitting and the absorption of new personnel. With minor exception, its units had not been involved in any fighting on the Western front since early November, and therefore not been identified by the usual method of combat patrols, prisoners and so on.

Now it was estimated that the Sixth was Rundstedt's armoured reserve to be used in any counter-attack he decided upon. But where was the Sixth?

In early December, Allied intelligence carried the headquarters of the Sixth on its situation maps in the vicinity of Cologne, and assigned at least five uncommitted Panzer divisions to Dietrich's command. But the actual location of Dietrich's troops was a matter of debate and conjecture. General Sibert, intelligence chief of Bradley's Twelfth Army Group, thought it might be concentrated around Bielefeld to the north-east of Cologne. Colonel 'Monk' Dickson, First Army's scholarly-looking Chief-of-Intelligence, placed it rather indefinitely between the rivers Roer and Rhine. Patton's intelligence chief, Colonel Oscar Koch, guessed it was somewhere between Cologne and Düsseldorf. The US Ninth Army apparently did not want to enter the guessing game and made no judgement about where Dietrich's SS might be. As for Eisenhower's Chief-of-Intelligence, the canny Scot Brigadier Kenneth Strong, he summed up the matter nicely in a report of 10 December. According to SHAEF Intelligence, 'There is no further news of the Sixth SS Panzer Army beyond vague rumours.'

Where was the missing army? It was sitting right under the noses of the Americans, directly opposite the axis between First Army's Vth and VIIIth Corps, in the dark, dripping fir woods of the Eifel on what the GIs who were stationed there had been calling these last three months the 'Ghost front'.

2

Nothing much had happened on the Ghost front since the second week of September 1944, when the men of the 28th US Infantry Division had crossed the border stream, the River Our, between Luxembourg and Germany. They had clambered up the steep wooded bank on the other side, confident that the Germans were on the run and that nothing would stop them; their war was almost over. 'Send the boys home by Christmas!' – that was the slogan now. At dawn on 13 September (an unlucky thirteenth for the 28th Division) the infantry ran straight into the first outposts of the German Siegfried Line. It stopped them dead. The next day was the same, and the next.

Their prisoners were under-aged youths and sick men from the German 'Stomach' battalions,* ill-trained and lacking in spirit for the most part; but, as Major James Ford, S–3 of the 28th's 110th Infantry Regiment pointed out, 'It doesn't

---

* Special battalions of men with stomach ailments grouped together for dietary reasons

matter what training a man may have when he is placed inside such protection as was afforded by the pillboxes. Even if he merely stuck his weapon through the aperture and fired occasionally, it kept our men from moving ahead freely.'

In the end the 28th gave up and, with the corps to which it belonged, withdrew from Germany, back across the Our, into Luxembourg. By the beginning of October 1944, an uneasy peace in the middle of a bloody war settled across these 85 miles of front.

Twisting and turning through rugged, lonely countryside, heavily wooded and furrowed by the two border rivers, the Our and the Sauer (Sûre in French), the front ran from Monschau (Germany) to Echternach in the south (Luxembourg). It was held by six American divisions, two of them veteran, but still nursing themselves after the battering they had received in the battle in the 'Green Hell of Hürtgen' – the 28th and 4th Infantry; one which was experienced and combat-ready, the 2nd Infantry; and three, the 99th Infantry, 9th Armoured and the 106th Infantry, all inexperienced – and, in the case of the 106th, the newest division of any Allied formation on any front throughout the world!

But for General Bradley, the Twelfth Army Group commander, this long, difficult front, held by shattered or green divisions, was a 'calculated risk'. A general couldn't concentrate his mass everywhere; he needed the bulk of his fighting troops to north and south of the Ghost front, where 'a shooting war' was actually taking place. Besides, everyone knew that the Germans would never take the offensive; and even if they *did*, would they choose the difficult, wooded terrain of the Ardennes in winter for an armoured thrust? *No sir!*

So from the end of September 1944, the Ghost front had settled into a kind of limbo, a haven of peace in the midst of war. Here the artillery fired mainly for the sake of registration, and patrols probed the enemy lines on the other side of the twin rivers only to keep in practice. Within rifle range of each other on the height on both sides of the river line, German observers could watch the Amis line up for chow; and Americans watched the German women from the occupied German villages, viewed on the skyline, sneak into the bunkers of the Siegfried Line to pass the long, boring nights with the soldiers manning them. Here it was live and let live, with both sides resting and watching and avoiding irritating each other by anything which might be considered a warlike action.

Yet, in spite of the static nature of the war on the Ghost front, the more fearful or sensitive of that handful of veterans and mass of greenhorns manning the long front experienced a sense of unease and foreboding as November gave way to December. After the early snowfalls up in the line when an army of skeletal, brooding black firs stood out against the glittering white ground, such soldiers might feel an unreasoning desire to escape to the rear, back to the safety of the little villages huddled around the slate-roofed churches in the valleys.

Even here, though, they couldn't feel quite at ease. Here the villagers in their faded blue overalls and the women, mostly in a funereal black, spoke German. Outside their homes and shops, the Allied flags and pictures of Roosevelt, Churchill and King Leopold of Belgium, seen everywhere else in the towns and villages to the rear, were absent. Inside, in the heavily Teutonic atmosphere of the living rooms, the photographs of absent menfolk showed them, not in the familiar khaki of the Allied armies, but in the field-grey of the enemy.

For Luxembourg and the three eastern cantons of Belgium – Eupen, Malmédy and St Vith – which made up the US First Army's rear area, had been incorporated into the Reich in 1940, and most of the able-bodied men had been recruited into the Wehrmacht.*

Now, with the members of the Belgian resistance movement, the White army, in charge, which had mainly been recruited in the French-speaking parts of Belgium, and with denunciations, charges and counter-charges the order of the day, neighbour viewed neighbour with suspicion. Villages, and even families, were divided between those who felt

---

*From 1815 to 1920, the east cantons had been part of Prussia and later imperial Germany, so that most of the older people in the area had been born German. Similarly, Luxembourg had been under semi-Prussian control from 1815 to 1866.

themselves to be Belgian and those who still adhered to the German cause. After all, a good percentage of the local population was still evacuated or working in Germany, and nearly 27,000 men were members of the German armed forces. As a result, a strange, foreboding atmosphere hung over the rear, half-sullen, half-friendly, with every now and again small, mysterious incidents taking place, which only much later could be fitted into the jigsaw of events which preceded the great surprise attack. But by then, it was much too late to do anything about them.

In the first week of December 1944, Major Ralph Hill, in charge of civilian affairs in what was now the US 99th Infantry Division's area, was a frustrated man. For nearly two months he had been trying to cope, with a staff of eight, with the mass of problems left by the retreating Germans and the new ones occasioned by the arrival of the new 99th Division. In September he had evacuated 10,000 civilians to the rear. One month later he had been allowed to bring many of the more trust-worthy of them back to look after the rear area. But how was he to feed them? The Belgians, in what the locals called 'Old Belgium', refused to send up food to these 'traitors' on the frontier. In November, the harassed Major rounded up 10,000 cows and set up twelve butchering centres throughout his area.

Again, how was he to keep in touch with his various centres? He couldn't use military telephone lines, and the roads were constantly clogged with military traffic. In the end Hill had a brainwave. Why not use the old civilian telephone system?

In the basement of the post office in the border village of Büllingen, 5 miles behind the front, he discovered a large number of telephone terminals. Hurriedly, Hill attached a field telephone and rang each one in turn to check if they still worked.

They did. Suddenly a female voice came through loud and clear. '*Hier Bonn!*' the operator said in perfect German.

Hill, too startled by the announcement to comprehend fully that he was talking to an enemy civilian a good 100 miles behind the German front, 'made some chit-chat for a while'.

Then the German operator informed the American Major that her board said he appeared to be calling from Spa, to his rear, and rang off. Still bemused by the strange occurrence, Hill arranged to have the line cut and connected to the First Army's switchboard. It was only years later that he realized the full significance of the uncanny conversation. The Germans still had a communications link, not only with the villages of the east cantons immediately behind the front, but also with Spa, the Headquarters of General Hodges' First Army! What if they had an agent in place there? He would be able to communicate directly with his bosses in the Reich, as would any other spy the Germans had on the Ghost Front!

Ten miles away from Büllingen that same first week of December, farmer Peter Schaus, one of the few civilians to remain behind in the village of Recht, also experienced something rather peculiar. One midday a handful of American soldiers strolled into the village and asked Schaus to show them the houses abandoned by villagers who had fled into 'Old Belgium'. Schaus, who was also a rural councillor, showed them willingly enough. The Amis were always generous with their cigarettes, and he was getting a bit sick of smoking home-made weed, sprayed with 'Virginia Odour' to give it a bit of flavour.

According to the Ami, who spoke broken German, they were looking for billets; but it struck Schaus, who was no fool, that the Amis were not particularly interested in the abandoned farmhouses and cottages, and that most of them did not speak a single word all the time they were with him. Before they left, their spokesman gave Schaus a cigar for his trouble, something which puzzled him. For the Amis rewarded civilians with one of their excellent Lucky Strikes or Camels. As yet he had never even seen an American smoke a cigar. In the end Schaus concluded they were deserters who were looking for some place behind the front where they 'could take a dive', as the slang of the day had it.

But Peter Schaus, smart as he was, was mistaken this time. At ten o'clock on the morning of 17 December 1944, one day after the great surprise attack had started, two of those self-same Amis knocked at Peter Schaus's door once more.

This time, with a huge grin, they identified themselves in fluent German and informed the perplexed farmer that they were Skorzeny-Leute.*

That same week strange Amis turned up asking for information at the villages of Poteau, Kaiserbaracke, Andler and a score of hamlets in the east cantons. Later they'd appear again, this time speaking German instead of English. One told Miss Sophia Lejeune in Kaiserbaracke that he had been on the road behind the Ami lines for six weeks, but wouldn't say where he had been. Another, dressed still in Ami uniform, greeted Mrs Muesch-Margraff, a widow living in Poteau, with a grin and 'Heil Hitler', and cried out as he saw the look of astonishment on her face, 'SS voran!' †

It was no different in the western areas of Luxembourg. At night Germans would occasionally appear on the American side of the rivers Our–Sauer, to take their pleasure with the local German-speaking farm wenches. They would tell the girls that they were from the Siegfried Line positions on the other side, but how they got across the rivers and through the Ami positions they would not explain.‡

Captain Robert Merriam, US Army historian with the Ninth Army, was driving through Luxembourg that year along the River Our with a guide, who told him: 'Have to be careful at night. Krauts like to sneak patrols over just to make a social call. Ambushed a jeep in daylight the other day and got a new battalion commander. Hell, he didn't even get a chance to report in.'

A little later his guide delivered Captain Merriam to a friend with a line company who was on the range with his men. But it was no ordinary range. Its backstop was the front, the River Our, and it was under sporadic shellfire from the German side, even as the infantrymen fired their rifles at the targets.

---

*Skorzeny's people
†'SS to the front!'
‡ They came across by hidden culverts. When the great surprise attack came, a whole battalion of the attacking 5th German Parachute Division used one such culvert to slip across completely unnoticed.

'Nearly had some trouble just before you came,' his friend drawled quietly. 'God-damned Jerries must be using poor grade ammunition. Anyway they had a short and it dropped right behind the targets. The boys out there were in the pits and none of them was hurt, so I said, "Mark those targets". There were nine jagged shell-fragment holes in the bull's-eye. Pretty damned good shooting for a Kraut!'

As Captain Merriam concluded ruefully, 'That was the phoney front!'

On the afternoon of Friday, 15 December 1944, Cy Peterman, the veteran war correspondent of the Philadelphia *Inquirer*, also visited that same sector of the Ghost front in Luxembourg in search of a story. He didn't get much, for nothing ever seemed to happen there, and he came away with the tale of 1,700 German civilians hiding out in a cave used for growing mushrooms.

Driving along what the GIs called 'Skyline Drive', the ridge road on the American-held bank of the River Our, a position completely exposed to any observer on the German side, he was overcome by a feeling of foreboding. On the way down he had seen no sign of the Germans. Now he could see the tiny figures in field-grey quite clearly, and some of them seemed to be moving bridging equipment down the wooded slopes to the banks of the Our. Trucks were grinding their way down the fire-breaks and forest trails, too.

Finally, his own jeep was spotted. There was the thump of enemy cannon. The still afternoon air was torn apart by the whine of shellfire. In quick succession three shells slammed into the hillside above the road.

Bolton, Peterman's jeep driver, did not need a second invitation to get going. He floored the accelerator and ripped the wheel round. A few moments later Peterman found himself bouncing up and down on the shell-pocked road that led away from the 'Skyline Drive' leading to St Vith, in the direction of Clervaux.

A little while afterwards, Bolton, ashen-faced, ventured back on to the main Luxembourg–St Vith road, and they passed through the latter township, now the headquarters of the newly arrived 106th Division. The population didn't look

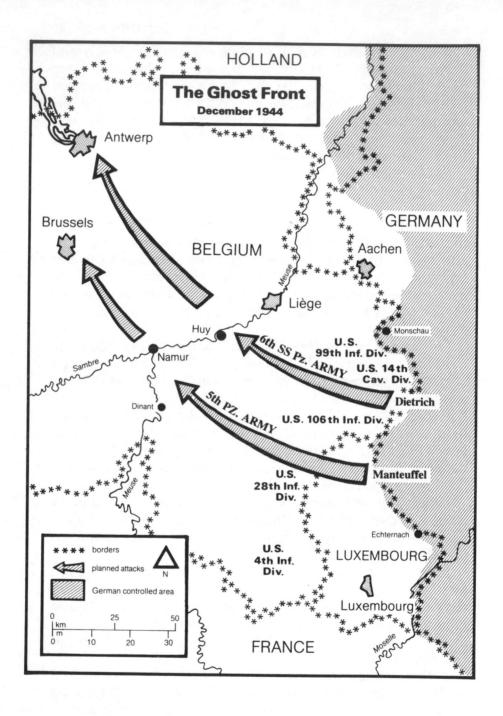

The Ghost Front
December 1944

HOLLAND

GERMANY

Antwerp

Brussels

BELGIUM

Aachen

Meuse

Liège

Huy

U.S.
99th Inf. Div.

Monschau

Sambre

Namur

6th SS Pz. ARMY

U.S. 14th
Cav. Div.

Dinant

5th PZ. ARMY

Dietrich

U.S. 106th Inf. Div.

Manteuffel

U.S.
28th Inf.
Div.

Echternach

U.S.
4th Inf.
Div.

LUXEMBOURG

Luxembourg

Meuse

★ ★ ★ ★ borders

N

↞ planned attacks

German controlled area

FRANCE

Moselle

0   km   25   50
0   10   20   30
m

46

too friendly, and Peterman had the distinct impression that the civilians 'glowered' at him as they headed slowly out of town on the Malmedystrasse.

Some time later Peterman presented himself to General Hodges, the First Army Commander, a general he had known for several years. Courtney Hodges, a sad-faced, craggy general whose pace was that of the infantryman he had once been in the First World War, received the newspaperman in his office at the Hôtel Britannique, where in 1918 Field Marshal Hindenburg had decided that he must tell his Kaiser that Germany had lost the war and would have to surrender.

Here, over a drink, Peterman told Hodges of his experiences on the way back: the busy Germans, the bridging equipment, the shells, the sullen looks of the local populace, and how tenuously the Ghost front was being held.

Hodges was not normally a worrier, but he, too, had begun to be concerned about the situation on the Ghost front. 'I'll see what we can get for reinforcements,' he told Peterman, 'but I doubt if it will be much.'

Casualties in the rifle companies had been heavy, he knew. Indeed, in the morning General Eisenhower would meet with General Bradley at the former's HQ in Paris to discuss this urgent problem, and there was already talk of a five-per-cent levy on non-combat outfits to raise the necessary men. Some people had even suggested that Negro troops might be used, though the situation, in Hodges' opinion, was not grave enough to warrant such a radical measure.*

As they parted, Hodges muttered that all he had to put into the Ghost front area in the way of reinforcements were a camouflage and chemical outfit. But General Hodges knew something that Peterman did not, something which he dared not breathe a word about even to his intimates. If the worst came to the worst on the thinly defended Ghost front and the Germans did attack, Hodges knew that his 'Secret Limeys' would warn him in time.

---

* In December 1944 the US army was still strictly segregated, with only two black tank battalions in the whole of the European theatre of operations.

3

In the latter years of the war any observant visitor to one of the major US headquarters throughout the European theatre of operations might well spot them. A truck, a handful of tents, and perhaps a van bristling with aerials, discreetly tucked away in an orchard or behind some small barn, and all manned by men in the blue of the British Royal Air Force. 'What,' the observant visitor might well ask, 'were Air Force men, British to boot, and mostly of lowly rank, doing at an American higher army headquarters where full colonels were a dime a dozen?'

'There was the little truck hidden among the trees,' a US Air Force officer, Lewis Powell, noticed in North Africa, 'with people occasionally going to and fro. I thought it was a Direction-Finding Unit.' In Normandy, frustrated headquarters clerks at Bradley's HQ, unable to make out the identity of these strange Britishers in their midst, christened them the 'Secret Limeys'.

Who were they, and how was it they always had immediate access to the top US commanders, such as Bradley, Hodges or Patton, even if their rank was that of a mere pilot officer?

They called themselves 'SLUs', which stood for 'Special Liaison Units,' which gave no clue to what form their special liaison took, which was wise. For these low-ranking men, and women, in the blue of the Royal Air Force bore with them the most important Allied secret of the whole long war, one that hundreds of quite ordinary men and women kept until their chief, Group-Captain Freddie Winterbotham, exiled in that remote Devonshire farmhouse of his, finally revealed it to the astonished world in 1974.*

It is recorded that a quarter of a century after she had been in charge of Field Marshal Alexander's Intelligence War

---

*When I first visited him there in 1973 and urged him to publish his knowledge, which he did the year following in his book *The Ultra Secret*, he told me over homemade wine in his study, that his former colleagues of the Secret Intelligence Service would put him in the Tower of London 'for a hundred years'. He was then approaching eighty.

Room in Italy, one such devoted initiate, Judy Hutchinson, was rushed to Oxford's Churchill Hospital suffering from a brain haemorrhage. Her condition was critical, and only a long operation saved her life. But all the time, while she was in great pain and anxiety, her over-riding concern was that she might give away that tremendous secret in her delirium.

What was that overwhelming secret?

It was the Ultra Secret, the most comprehensive and effective system for penetrating an enemy's mind that has ever been evolved. In the thirty-three centuries of recorded espionage there had never been anything like it; and it may safely be said that the espionage war – and all that resulted from winning that war in the shadows – was won not in the shabby backstreets of Berlin or Hamburg by sinister Allied agents and their bought creatures, but by a handful of elderly Oxford dons in a rusty tin hut in the middle of the peaceful English Home Counties.

The saga of what Winston Churchill called his 'most secret sources' in his own account of the Second World War (he never identified them any further) began in the late 1920s when the German Reichswehr adopted a mechanical coding device named 'the Enigma' as the basis of its top secret signals. The machine itself looked like a primitive typewriter, save for one thing: when the operator pressed key 'A', for example, the letter 'A' was not typed, but, say, 'F'. How? It was all done by highly elaborate electric wiring and rotors which could produce a great many permutations, so that its inventor and later developer, Dutchman Hugo Alexander Koch and German Dr Arthur Scherbius, thought that the coded message which the Enigma produced was absolutely unbreakable. Indeed, when the British finally tackled the Enigma problem, one cryptanalyst, Peter Calvocorcssi, calculated that the possible permutations of the final version of the machine reached an astronomic figure of nearly six thousand million million million.

In the early thirties the Poles first took up the challenge. Their military intelligence managed to steal and buy several of the German Enigmas, and set about the problem of speedy deciphering of the messages they could send. In the mid-thirties, French intelligence, with whom the Poles had always worked closely, offered to help with money and other resources. By 1937 the Poles, and indirectly the French, were breaking the German messages, but it was a frustrating and lengthy business in spite of the fact they had developed the 'bomba', once described as 'like a mad scientist's console from an old Fritz Lang horror film'. This high-speed calculating mechanism, which was no more than a primitive forerunner of the sophisticated ones later used by the British and Americans, did make it possible for the Poles to tackle the Enigma's problems at speeds far beyond the scope of human thought.

In July 1939, with the Second World War only weeks away, British intelligence's own highly skilled decoding branch finally got into the act, with Commander Alexander Denniston's Code and Cipher School, mockingly called by its members 'the Golf Club and Chess Society'. Denniston, whose son called him 'the most secretive man I've ever known',* went to Warsaw with Dillwyn Knox, a celebrated World War I cryptanalyst (who had helped to break the famed Zimmermann Telegram which helped to bring the United States into World War I), plus a certain 'Colonel Sandwich', as an observer.

There it was agreed to have one of the German Enigmas brought to London in the diplomatic bag, and thus on the evening of 16 August 1939, the top-secret machine arrived by courier at Victoria Station to be met personally by 'Colonel Sandwich' himself wearing full evening dress with the rosette of the Legion of Honour. It was, as Eisenhower's Chief-of-Intelligence Brigadier Kenneth Strong would say forty years later, 'Colonel Sandwich's' 'greatest achievement of the whole war'. Who was 'Colonel Sandwich'? None other than Colonel Stewart Menzies, the future head of the British Secret Intelligence Service!

In 1940, after Poland and France had been submerged and Britain was on its own, completely cut off from intelligence from the Continent, Denniston's Code and Cipher School, evacuated to a red-brick mansion at Bletchley Park, worked feverishly to find a more efficient and speedier substitute

---

* To the author

for the Bomba – and they succeeded with an early form of the computer called by the staff at Bletchley the 'Green Goddess'.

It was about this time that 'Zero C', Group Captain Winterbotham, a long-time member of the Secret Intelligence Service, came on the scene. He decided that these top-secret intercepts, of which ex-SIS man Malcolm Muggeridge said later '[they] had the rarity value of the Dead Sea Scrolls', had to be protected. In his forthright way he told 'C', Menzies now Major-General, 'This can't go on. The whole op will be blown in a few months if we don't control it properly.'

'C' agreed, and Winterbotham set up his first Special Liaison Unit. Headed by a junior officer named Humphries, it consisted of three sergeants. Its duties were to attach itself to a battle headquarters, where it would receive the Ultra (as the new top-secret coding was called) information from Bletchley by means of a one-time pad.* (Both sender and receiver have a pad of tear-off sheets, each of which contains specific ciphering data. The sender having indicated the relevant page, the sender uses his own copy to decipher the signal he has received and then destroys the page he has just used.) The Ultra information would then be taken personally by the officer in charge of the SLU to the commanding general or his deputy. The latter would be allowed to read and digest the message, but the actual message form would have to be handed to the SLU officer for destruction afterwards.

Thereafter Winterbotham personally selected several score of such crews for duty all over the world, binding them to life-long secrecy, interviewing them in the presence of another officer who guarded the door with a drawn loaded revolver in his hand to emphasize the absolute seriousness of the interview! Later, as more and more US units came to Europe, certain of their commanding generals were let into the secret – Clark, Patton, Hodges and Bradley among them – and special US officers were trained by the British as 'Ultra

---

* Later, the one-time pad would be replaced by the Typex machine, a form of ciphering system similar to the Enigma. When one was lost in France by a careless US army crew, Eisenhower instituted a personal search to find the lost truck which was carrying it. It was never found.

Advisers' to be attached to major US headquarters. So it was that when General Hodges took over the command of the US First Army in France in 1944, he, his Chief-of-Intelligence Colonel Dickson, his Ultra Adviser Captain Adolph Rosengarten, and the handful of men in the British SLU were the only people in that 200,000-strong army who knew the secret.

Ultra served them well in a dozen different ways; indeed, its information probably saved Hodges' First from disaster in the first week of August 1944 when Bletchley warned General Hodges that Hitler had ordered an all-out attack towards the beaches. With a four-division armoured strike force, his soldiers would smash through Hodges' First Army and reach Avranches on the coast, there cutting Hodges off from Patton's Third Army now deep into Brittany.

Forewarned, Hodges was ready and waiting, backed up by the 9th Tactical Air Command. At Mortain, General Hobbs's 30th Infantry Division held out against all that the Germans could throw at them, while the Lightnings and Mustangs of General Quesada's 9th Tactical Air Command pulverised von Kluge's armour. By the afternoon of the first day of the great counter-attack, the German seventh Army was signalling 'the actual attack has been at a standstill since 1300 hours owing to the employment by the enemy of a great number of fighter-bombers.' Within days it was over and the enemy had been defeated. Hodges had had his first victory of the campaign – thanks to Ultra.

And so it went on right throughout that mad rush across France, Belgium and Holland towards the frontiers of the Reich. General Hodges knew the contents of the messages sent by Enigma to German commanders from the OKW* as soon as did their recipients. But as the Germans began to fall back across their own frontiers, a change began to take place. Now there was no longer such a great need for the Enigma. The Wehrmacht could begin to use a wide network of safe telephone and teleprinter links which the 'Boffins of Bletchley' could not tap. Less radio meant less Ultra. There was one exception, however – the Luftwaffe, which still used

---

* The German High Command

the Enigma to a great degree. Thus it was on 17 November 1944, that Bletchley picked up from the Luftwaffe circuit a detailed account of all that service's top-secret jet aircraft and their code-names, as well as a great deal of priceless technological data.

Yet the German army stubbornly refused to go on the air and reveal what it was up to, for Hitler had ordered a strict wireless blackout. Air reconnaissance helped little, for all troop movement took place under the cover of darkness. Sixteen OSS agents, all captured German prisoners-of-war 'volunteers', were dropped over the Rhineland armed with the new 'Joan-Eleanor' ('J-E'), a greatly expanded form of the walkie-talkie which enabled the agent to talk to the radio operator in a special adapted British Mosquito fighter-bomber at a height of 30,000 feet – but produced no results. Only four returned. The rest probably surrendered immediately to the police once they reached the ground.

Some of the officers connected with Ultra, such as Hodges' Ultra Adviser Captain Adolph Rosengarten and Colonel Ewart, who handled intelligence at Field Marshal Montgomery's advance HQ, suspected that something was going on in Germany but they could not ascertain exactly what it was. Later, Rosengarten and Ewart met to mull over what information they had possessed before the deluge burst upon them. Had they overlooked anything? they asked themselves. From Ultra, thanks to Hitler's edict, there had come virtually nothing, they concluded.

Again the Luftwaffe slipped up. Its radio security was generally regarded by Allied experts as sloppier than that of the other services. Thus it was that on 16 November an Enigma message was picked up at Bletchley and in due course passed on to all top commanders, including Eisenhower, Bradley, Montgomery and, it is believed, Hodges (at all events Hodges would have heard of it from his boss Bradley). It came from a Luftwaffe 'FLIVO', an air liaison officer. In this message there was some reference to a *'Jägeraufmarsch'* (fighter-plane concentration) and 'an imminent big operation'. In itself, there was nothing particularly remarkable in the text, though that one word, *'Jägeraufmarsch'*, was always used before major attacks – save for one thing. The unknown FLIVO who had sent the message was the air liaison officer to the 'missing army', von Rundstedt's armour strike force, Sepp Dietrich's Sixth SS Panzer Army.

THREE

Die Wacht am Rhein

1

On Monday, 11 September 1944, a young American sergeant, Warner Holzinger, stood on the western bank of the River Our, which marked the border between Luxembourg and Germany, and stared at a wrecked bridge across the Our. Only hours before the fleeing Germans had destroyed it and disappeared into the Eifel hills beyond. Now Staff-Sergeant Holzinger of the 5th US Armoured Division wondered whether he should follow them.

Nothing disturbed the silence on the other side. To his left the tiny German hamlet of Gemünd seemed abandoned, and the steep fir-covered hill, that rose a sheer five hundred feet from the river, also appeared devoid of life.

Holzinger made a decision which gained for him a footnote in the histories of World War II. He ordered his little patrol to cross the Our. As the night shadows started to race down the tight valley, Holzinger lead his men – Corporal Ralph Driver, Privates Locke and McNeath, plus the French guide Delille – across the waist-deep river.

A minute or two later, the five of them stood on the other side a little apprehensively, staring at the bunkers of the West Wall* that had been cunningly dug into the eastern bank. They were empty. The Germans had flown. Holzinger con-

---

* For the curious, those bunkers, wrecked now, are still there, hidden in the thick undergrowth.

sidered for a moment whether or not he should go back. There was an odd, ominous silence about this lonely place, dominated on both sides by the brooding green heights. In the end duty triumphed, and Sergeant Holzinger and his four men plodded up the height towards what looked like a straggle of abandoned, white-painted farm buildings.

The buildings were not what they seemed. Obviously hastily abandoned only hours before, they were the main bunkers of that famed Siegfried Line, on which the British Tommies had boasted five long years before they would hang their 'washing, mother dear'. The four Americans and one Frenchman had penetrated the Siegfried Line without a shot having been fired!

For a few moments they scouted around the twenty-odd concrete bunkers, against one of which someone had built a very unmilitary chicken coop in the years since they had last been permanently occupied. Then they had seen enough. The sun had already vanished. Now the heights were a stark, eerie black. Ten minutes later they were back on the Luxembourg side of the river, hurrying to their waiting scout-car. Thirty minutes after that they were reporting their exciting discovery that the vaunted Siegfried Line was empty and Germany was wide open to the 85th Reconnaissance Squadron's intelligence officer. An hour later, their army commander, General Courtney Hodges, knew that Germany had been pierced at last.

As the dry unemotional prose of the time had it: 'At 1805 hours on 11 September, a patrol led by Staff Sergeant Warner W. Holzinger crossed into Germany near the village of Stolzembourg, a few miles north-east of Vianden, Luxembourg.' Hitler's Reich, it seemed, was beaten at last!

On the same day, however, when Germany seemed almost at the end of its tether, a thousand miles away in occupied Norway, a 500-ton German U-boat, the U-507, commanded by Lieutenant Herrle, set sail from the port of Hammerfest on yet another secret mission in a war that had been fought in the Arctic Circle for these last four years. In its lean, grey belly it contained the men who would contribute materially to ensuring that soon that Ghost front would erupt into violence and sudden death.

Yet there was nothing very warlike about the men who made up the U-507's 'super-cargo' as it started its long journey northwards through a perfect blue sea. Most of them, admittedly, wore uniforms, but they were all technicians, and their leader was a civilian, Dr Wilhelm Dege, a bespectacled geographer now turned meteorologist. For Dr Dege's handful of young men, equipped with 1,800 cases of equipment and supplies, enough for two years' stay in the Arctic, were not going to fight with their hands but with their brains.

Since 1915, when, for the first time in history, weather reporting became an essential part of military campaigning, accurate weather forecasting had become part and parcel of every operation. Each bombing raid, every naval action, commando raid, parachute drop over enemy territory throughout World War II depended upon reliable information about the weather – and the weather in Western Europe could be accurately forecast only if the military meteorologists had prior information from the Arctic Circle.

Since early 1940, therefore, secret German teams had made their way to the Arctic Circle to ensure that Berlin received this information. For four years a lonely, strange war was fought all over the Arctic in wild, treacherous conditions between the Germans on one side and, at varying times, Russians, Danes, Norwegians, Britons, Canadians and Americans on the other. It was a cat-and-mouse campaign, small groups of highly skilled and tough men, hunting each other through the snow and ice, with the Allies trying to root out each new secret radio station which sent the vital information back to the German High Command in Berlin.

In all, the Germans sent out sixteen successful expeditions, in addition to setting up a large number of robot weather stations. These, planted by U-boats or dropped by aircraft, radioed back air and sea temperatures, wind speeds and directions and other information, and were so cleverly camouflaged that some of them were still operating long after Berlin had capitulated.

One by one, however, all these expeditions were rounded up by the Danish Sledge Patrol and the American Coast

Guard responsible for East Greenland and neighbouring waters; the British and Norwegians in charge of Jan Mayen and the Svalbard Archipelago; and the Russians, who kept watch on Franz Josef Land. Thus it was that Dr Dege was now under way at this late stage in the war – 'at the hour before zero', as the Germans were already calling this eleventh hour – to establish Germany's last secret weather station in the Arctic.

He had picked, as he wrote later himself, 'the island of Nordostland off Spitzbergen, nearly 15,000 square kilometres in size and regarded as one of the toughest areas in the whole of the Arctic'. Dege knew he had to reach the area by 15 September. Lieutenant Herrle informed Dege that unfortunately six or seven British destroyers were waiting for them off the west coast of Spitzbergen. Ultra had picked up the German Admiralty's signals from Kiel to Norway. So they decided to make a run for it along the very difficult east coast of that island.

Almost at once they bumped into a huge Allied convoy off Bear Island, bound for Murmansk with supplies for the Red army. Somehow they managed to escape from it, and arrived safely off the east coast of Spitzbergen to find, as Dege recorded later, 'a situation that had not occurred for over a hundred years – the area was completely free of ice'.

Luck was on their side. It made their task of establishing a base camp far easier. Dege, who had the use of the U-boat for two weeks, set his own men and the submariners to work. They erected the weather station, piled up their load of stores and even built a sauna, while Dege himself took the opportunity of rowing right round the island area, thus becoming the first scientist to do so. He returned to find the U-boat ready to set sail back to Norway. As he recorded laconically, 'Now we were alone.'

They were. In mid-October, the sun dipped below the horizon and bade goodbye till the following March, leaving the little camp in darkness to face the anger of a polar winter, some 600 miles below the North Pole. Here, on the roof of the world, Dege and his men started radioing regular weather reports back to the Reich. In a polar night which would last

127 days until the sun appeared again at the beginning of March 1945 and they were discovered by Allied radio-detector experts, they passed on the vital information which would decide all German military operations in north-western Europe.

By the middle of November 1944, Dege's team began sending back the readings and information that the Chief Executive Officer of the Reich's Meteorological Service, Dr Karl Recknagel, needed. He continued his work in that remote, secret base until finally he received the dubious honour of being the commander of the last German unit to surrender in World War II to the Allies, more than three months after the Wehrmacht had capitulated, at midnight on 3 September 1945.

In Berlin, however, Recknagel and his scientific team worked hard, assessing Dege's data in the light of the fact that the area of the Ghost front presented special problems. The climate of the Eifel-Ardennes was usually very rainy in November and December, with frequent, heavy mists lasting well into the late morning. Moreover, precise predictions by military meteorolgists were difficult, because the Ardennes lay directly on the boundary between the north-western and central European climatic zones. As a result, the climate there is affected by the conjunction of weather moving east from the British Isles and the Atlantic with that moving westward out of Russia.

Dr Karl Recknagel was an old hand at predicting the weather for his Führer. He had a habit of displaying his gold pocket watch and remarking that it had been 'given me by the Führer in person for my hundred-per-cent accurate weather forecasts before the Norwegian campaign' in April 1940. Late in November 1944, as confident as ever in spite of his many failures to forecast the weather correctly during the Russian campaign, he made his prediction. There would be rain, fog, mist and probably heavy snow in the last two weeks of December. It was the kind of weather the Führer would need to conceal his final preparations for the offensive from Allied air reconnaissance, and it would be the type of weather, too, which would later protect German ground forces from the feared Allied *Jabos* (dive-bombers). Recknagel even hazarded a guess when the real 'Führer weather'* as it was called, would commence. The date he gave was 16 December 1944. It was a date accepted by the German High Command's planning staff.

Now the proposed attack was given its final identity: it was allotted the cover-name '*Wacht am Rhein*' ('Watch on the Rhine'). The choice was brilliant, for if any Allied agent discovered it, he would assume it was basically a defensive action on the Rhine. '*Wacht am Rhein*' would commence on the morning of Saturday, 16 December 1944.

By the time that Dr Dege, in the hidden meteorological station on that remote Arctic island, radioed his vital finding to Berlin, Operation 'Watch on the Rhine' was in full swing. All along the front facing the Americans of the Ghost front the most stringent precautions were introduced to maintain secrecy. All units to be used in the first wave on that Saturday were forbidden to make any kind of reconnaissance. Potential deserters were warned off by the edict issued by Himmler himself that the family of any man deserting to the enemy would automatically be arrested and sent to a concentration camp. Movement took place only at night, across roads covered with straw, so that the vehicles would make the least possible noise. Smokeless fuel was issued to the troops. Each individual road had a 'road commander' in charge of it, who gave directions and instructions so that there was no need for the usual jumble of military road signs, indicating command posts, aid stations, unit shelters and the like. Top commanders played their role in the great deception, too. Field Marshal Model was reported to have dressed as a colonel so that his presence would not be remarked upon by the local people at Münstereifel. His Fifth Army commander, diminutive, ex-gentleman jockey General Hasso von Manteuffel, who had ordered that the tyres should be shot out on any vehicle moving by daylight in his area, took himself off to a café next to the border of Germany with Luxembourg. There

---

*There were two kinds of 'Führer weather': brilliant sunshine and heat for parades; rain and mist for offensive operations when faced with superior enemy air power.

he talked loudly about coming operations in a far-off section of the front in the hope that some local citizen might be working for the Americans and pass on the misleading information to them.

Now, disguised as a colonel of infantry (he had done a quick change and moved to a more modest staff car), he turned up at a divisional headquarters on the River Our. He told the general that he was reconnoitring a route for the relief of another division in the Siegfried Line, and asked if he might have permission to talk to the general's battalion commanders. The general, who did not recognise the disguised Army commander, grandly gave his permission, so off went the 'Colonel' to spend twelve hours at the front, questioning officers and men, especially those who had just come back from patrols behind the American lines on the Ghost front. Basically his question was always the same: 'What are the habits of the Amis?'

The answers they gave were very reassuring. The Americans on the Ghost front seemed to consider the area as a kind of rest camp, with nine-to-five hours. Every night the American GIs manning the line would remain on alert for one hour exactly after darkness; thereupon they would return to their winterised squad huts for the night. An hour before dawn their officers would stand them to. They would shave and wash and move into the line again, to see – as usual – nothing happening on the German side. But at night, so the infantrymen informed the disguised von Manteuffel, the front was German – totally. Before the ban on patrolling came into force they had been able to penetrate for miles into American-held territory with almost complete impunity. Once, they told him, they had even 'kidnapped' an American Sherman tank, all 30 tons of it, and brought it safely back to their own lines! It was the kind of good news that had already been relayed back to Obersturmbannführer Otto Skorzeny by his agents in Belgium and Luxembourg and passed on to that strange collection of men, recruited from all over Hitler's diminishing empire and from every branch of the German service, who were now being trained for their secret mission in a remote camp in Bavaria.

2

The whole operation had started with a mess. At one o'clock on the morning of 26 October, the signals duty clerk at the rear headquarters of Model's Army Group 'B' near Krefeld was alerted by the characteristic maybug-like burr of the teleprinter which linked the signals centre with the Führer's HQ. He snapped awake. The carriage began to move. Nothing important, just a few meaningless signs. Suddenly the text of a very startling message – in clear – began to appear.

It read,

VERY SECRET: To Divisional and Army Commands only. Officers and men who speak English are wanted for a special mission. The Führer has ordered the formation of a special unit of approximately two-battalion strength for use on the Western front in special operations and reconnaissance. Volunteers who are selected will report to Dienststelle Skorzeny* at Friedenthal.

It was signed by no less a person than Field Marshal Keitel.

The meaning of the message was crystal clear. Skorzeny was recruiting English-speaking soldiers and airmen for special operations, obviously behind Allied lines in the West. As soon as Skorzeny received the order, giving his name, the assembly area for the volunteers and the purpose of their mission in black and white, he lost his temper: he couldn't believe that anyone could be so foolish as to circulate it. Immediately he wanted to cancel the operation, for surely the Americans would pick up the order sooner or later. He ordered his adjutant to request the SS's liaison officer at the Führer's HQ, General Fegelein (Eva Braun's brother-in-law) to ask permission to have the operation cancelled. Fegelein refused. How could anyone approach Hitler and confess to him such a terrible blunder? No, Skorzeny would have to take his chances just like the rest of them committed to the great

---

* Skorzeny Company Office

surprise attack. Moodily Skorzeny agreed, telling himself that soon the Amis would know everything, and all his efforts would be meaningless.

In due course, American intelligence did pick up that amazing order. But equally amazingly they did nothing about it. According to General Bradley, who was questioned on the subject later, the message had indeed reached his head-quarters at Namur, but no one had taken much notice of it.

Now the first volunteers began to flood in, first to Friedenthal, and then to the Gräfenwöhr Training Ground in Bavaria, coming from all branches of the German Wehrmacht, even from the SS and the merchant marine.

One of the first to report was Sergeant Heinz Rohde, who was recovering from a bad wound and now serving as an instructor in a signals unit in Hamburg. He thought that he was heading for a cushy billet when he volunteered to get away from the almost daily raids on the shattered port. Soon he was going to change his mind. After a long and mysterious journey all over Germany, Sergeant Rohde found himself in the company of thirty other men from all branches of the service and ranging in rank from naval captain to air force lance-corporal at the country station at Rappenberg. Here, in the growing darkness, they were met by two SS officers. They warned the volunteers that their mission-to-be was top secret, and made them give up all their identity documents and other papers.

Now they went for a two-hour ride in lorries through the night, taking country trails, until at last they were unloaded at a camp, guarded by SS men armed with fixed bayonets. Rohde tried to talk to one of them while they waited in the cold darkness, but to no avail. As he recalled after the war, 'They were Ukrainian volunteers who didn't spcak a word of German. But one thing was clear from these guards. Once we passed through the big gate, there would be no turning back. We were leaving the real world behind us.'

They were. Almost immediately one of the volunteers was ordered to be shot for giving away the secret. He had sent a letter home, which had been intercepted, giving too full a description of their mission; this was contrary to the strict oath to remain absolutely silent on the subject which they had all sworn. Isolation was so severely maintained that the sick were not sent to hospital outside that remote camp, but tended as well as was possible in the sick bay. All men were dosed against influenza and colds.

Now tests were run to ascertain the degree of competence of the volunteers in English. Most of them were found to have exaggerated their knowledge of the language. They were retained to make up the bulk of what was now being called Panzerbrigade 150. Out of the 3,000-odd volunteers, however, some 200 were selected who really could speak English fluently. Most of them were sailors who had served in the American merchant marine before the war. Some were German-Americans who had lived in the States and possessed dual nationality. One or two had even served at one time or another in the US army.

These men were grouped together in a special unit named after its commander, Captain Stielau – the 'Stielau Unit' – which was kept separate from the rest of the brigade. Sergeant Rohde was one of those segregated from the rest. As he recalled later, 'Almost immediately I was struck by the unusual, almost unsoldierly attitude of the members of this unit. The tone was easy-going and very comradely, so that in an astonishingly short time we achieved a feeling of "togetherness" which you usually find only among soldiers in times of great stress at the front.'

The Stielau Unit started training at once. As Rohde remembered shortly after the war, 'At first we were mostly concerned with learning the idiom of the GIs. The performance of American films, especially war films, played a great role in our training. Then came short visits to American POW camps where we mixed with the GIs and gained the impression that we were developing into perfect Yankees!'

As November gave way to December, the men of the Stielau Unit were broken up into teams, nine in all, who would use American jeeps and American equipment to carry out sabotage, reconnaissance behind the enemy's lines, spread news of disaster and do everything possible to create panic and confusion behind the American front.

Each jeep would contain three or four men – a driver, a

commander, a saboteur or radio operator and an interpreter, the only one of the team who could speak perfect English.* In addition to their normal equipment these men carried a phial of prussic acid – the lethal pill or L-Pill – concealed in the wool of their cigarette lighters to be used to commit suicide in case they were captured.

In the first days of December, as the volunteers learned the tricks of close combat, sabotage, the use of plastic explosive and specially silenced machine pistols (a new German secret weapon), they were introduced to their new identities. As Rohde remembers, 'We were led into the quartermaster's clothing store which was piled high with all types of American uniform and told to kit ourselves out, from underpants on upwards.' Later, they were taken into another room and told to pick a suitable American identity document for each individual member of the teams. Accordingly, Heinz Rohde found himself transformed, somewhat unwillingly, into Sergeant Morris Woodahl of the US army. 'It was a very funny feeling,' he wrote later, 'somehow a little eerie, and we lost no time in hiding our American uniforms with German para-overalls and the little paratroop fatigue cap which went with it.'

With nearly 3,000 men locked away in a tight camp, forbidden to leave, their mail censored, their days spent trying to imitate Americans, naturally the rumours flew thick and fast. They were going to be dropped in US uniform to relieve the sizeable German garrisons still trapped in the Breton ports of Brest and Lorient. No, that wasn't the mission at all. Instead, they were to make a surprise attack on the great, sprawling US cage at Cherbourg, Camp 'Lucky Strike', as the Amis called it, which held many thousands of German prisoners waiting for shipment to the United States.

At first Skorzeny tried to kill the rumours. But soon he realised that the rumour-mongers would provide the cover for the real mission he needed, in case one of his men blabbed.

---

*Unknown to Captain Stielau, by grouping four men in a jeep he was already making his men objects of suspicion; for US Army Regulations insisted that, for safety reasons, only three men should ride in a jeep at any one time.

He decided to confirm the most extravagant of these wild rumours running through Grafenwoehr.

Then it happened, the incident which would plague Skorzeny for many years to come and which would result in General Eisenhower's becoming a prisoner in his own head-quarters, guarded by a full battalion of heavily armed military policemen. One morning a young officer, Lieutenant N. of the Stielau Unit, asked to have a private talk with Skorzeny. Very seriously he told the scar-faced giant, once they were alone, 'Obersturmbannführer, I think I know what the real objective is!'

Suddenly Skorzeny was all ears. Only two other officers in the whole camp knew the mission. Had one of them talked? Before Skorzeny could express his dismay, the young soldier continued, 'The Brigade is to march on Paris and capture Eisenhower's headquarters!'

Skorzeny forced himself not to laugh. 'So, so,' he said, with a significant frown.

That seemed to convince the lieutenant that he was cor-rect, for he said, 'May I offer you my co-operation, sir? I was stationed a long time in France and know Paris well. My French is good, too. You can rely on me. This is my plan.'

In a rush, the eager young soldier explained how the Brigade would enter Paris from various directions, posing as Americans, taking with them German tanks that they would maintain had been captured at the front and were being taken to the rear. They would meet somewhere central for the concentrated attack on Eisenhower's HQ.

Skorzeny pretended to go along with the scheme and said that he knew Paris, too, and had often sat in the Café de la Paix, sipping a drink.

With that he dismissed the young man, who naturally related his brilliant scheme to others of his comrades, giving the name of the café as their rendezvous. In years to come Skorzeny would live 'to regret ever mentioning that damned Café de la Paix'.

Nevertheless, in spite of the wild rumours while Captain Stielau's special unit began to shake down and was reaching a high degree of readiness for the coming operation, Skorzeny was still experiencing difficulties with the main body of his undercover outfit, Panzerbrigade 150.

Back in October he had been promised all the US equipment he required, but the German High Command had not taken into consideration the favour with which US equipment and vehicles, particularly the jeep, were regarded in German front-line units.

Every officer Skorzeny met seemed to have captured a jeep for his own private use. But on the day that Colonel-General Jodl issued his order calling in the little American vehicle in order that it could be sent to the new secret force, jeeps vanished from the face of the earth. In the end, he sent out his officers to forage for the elusive but highly prized jeep, which unknown to Skorzeny had gained its strange name from the average GI's unwillingness to pronounce its official one – 'General Purpose' (GP) – in full. To their surprise they found fifteen of them hidden in a barn.

It was the same with heavier US vehicles. Skorzeny had put in a request for twenty Sherman tanks, thirty armoured cars and vehicles for three battalions of motorised infantry. What he received were only two Shermans, six British armoured cars and about a dozen American half-tracks. In the end a harassed Skorzeny was forced to have German Panther tanks disguised as American ones. Sheet metal was added to various parts of the German tank to give it roughly the same outline as an American one, but as Skorzeny commented drily when he saw the first one, with its newly painted American star on its side, 'All I can say is that they can deceive only very young American troops, viewed at night, from very far away!'

It was little different with the thousands of American uniforms which were shipped to the camp to equip Panzerbrigade 150. Among the heaps of khaki-coloured clothing, there were hundreds of greatcoats, which were basically useless for Skorzeny; combat troops then usually wore field jackets in the line. Eventually the Quartermaster-General did send him a large number of these precious jackets, but they were found to be covered with prisoner-of-war triangles and the letters 'KG' (Kriegsgefangener, i.e. 'POW'). In the end Skorzeny told his men, 'Never matter, you can pick up all you want after the breakthrough.'

Now the training of the special brigade reached its final stages. Time was running out fast, and Skorzeny was already working furiously on the planning of his attack; for he already knew the assignments for both the Stielau Unit and his Brigade.

In spite of the fact that the knowledge of English among his Brigade was low, he and his instructors had managed to change the attitude of his pseudo-Americans. Skorzeny had reasoned that nationality was a matter of basic instincts, which expressed themselves in certain habits and attitudes. The German, he thought from his perspective as an easy-going Austrian, was stiff and wooden, especially if that German were a soldier to boot. He had broken down that woodenness. He had taught his men to slouch, chew gum, relax against walls with their hands in their pockets, something no good German soldier would dream of doing. Moreover, all of them had been taught a few key phrases if challenged, mostly profane. 'Go an' lay an egg,' was a favourite. 'So is your ol' man' was another. More persistent challengers were to be told bluntly, 'Go, crap in yer hat, buddy!'

But there was one problem that Skorzeny's instructors could not overcome, as the day of the Brigade's move drew ever closer and the rumours flew thick and fast about its mission: what would happen to them if they were taken prisoner dressed in American uniform and carrying American identification? They were told that the enemy had already violated the laws of war by bombing the civilian population of Germany, parachuting saboteurs and commandos behind German lines and fomenting partisan warfare in German-occupied countries. This kind of behaviour legitimised the wearing of American uniforms. However, to bolster up the morale of the worried troopers, their instructors explained that they were advised not to engage in combat while wearing American uniforms. *Just before they opened fire, they were recommended to change into German uniform!*

Of course, the suggestion was absurd, strictly a matter of form. Already, unknown to them the special units had been written off by the German High Command. Field Marshal von Rundstedt, the nominal commander of the Army in the West, when he heard of the new Brigade, and that it would use American uniform, told his Chief-of-Staff, General Westphal, to ask Colonel-General Jodl whether such an operation was 'fully in accordance with international law'. Jodl, pale-faced, cunning and highly intelligent, replied: 'Since the Field Marshal has raised the problems we have re-examined the matter. There is no question of any infringement of international law. It is merely a war stratagem, such as the other side has already used on all fronts with far greater frequency than we have. You need, therefore, have no scruples. Moreover, all the men selected arc volunteers. They are quite aware of the possibility that they may be treated as partisans. This they have accepted. No one has forced them into it.'

The inference was clear. If captured, Skorzeny's men were doomed – and the High Command knew it.

3

As always in his wartime career as spy-catcher and spy master, Lt Colonel Hermann Giskes was lucky. He had been lucky right from the start. The anti-tank unit which he would have joined if he had not been advised by an old crony to volunteer for the Abwehr instead had been shot to pieces in France in 1940. In the same year, travelling to meet one of his agents, the Dutchman Hooper, who had become a naturalised Englishman and betrayed his country for gold, he had been warned just before he crossed the border to Holland that Hooper intended to kill him and throw his body into a ditch. Again he had survived. His luck had held in the great retreat of the summer of 1944, and he had survived the purge of the Abwehr a little later. While his former chief Admiral Canaris now languished in Flossenburg concentration camp, waiting as a traitor to be strangled to death by chicken wire, and many of his old comrades of the Secret Service were in gaol or on the run, Giskes himself was still operational. His luck still held. He had been lucky right from the start with Operation 'Heinrich', the cover plan he had dreamed up immediately he had left Model's HQ that November day. It had gone smoothly from the beginning. Now it was in full swing and the results were pouring in.

He had begun with that problem raised by Model: how to get Allied civilians to work for Germany at a time when that country was obviously facing defeat. His fellow-intelligence officer summoned to come up with an idea had stated categorically that it was impossible. Giskes, the spy master, who had subverted so many men and women in these five years during the war-in-the-shadows, had not been so sure. It could be done, but how?

In the end, he played the old game of the spy master; he would make his agents think they were working for another power and not for Germany. Hadn't the British in the past convinced some of their working-class agents on the Continent that they were spying for the 'workers' and peasants' paradise' and not for perfidious, plutocratic Albion?

Accordingly, Colonel Giskes approached an engineer of his acquaintance, currently running a labour camp in the Eifel, not far from the Luxembourg border. Most of the workers in the camp were Belgians from the east cantons and Luxembourgers, who officially were classed as Reichsdeutsche (i.e. Germans) though behind their backs they were mocked as Beutedeutsche (i.e. booty or looted Germans). These Germans-by-capture were allowed to leave the camp during daylight hours to work under supervision, but their guards and, in particular, the engineer in charge, were suspicious of their motives. As Germany suffered defeat after defeat, their loyalty to the German cause grew increasingly weaker. Most of them simply wanted to get back home across the border before the final crash came and it was too late.

Naturally the engineer, a good loyal German, was horrified when Giskes made his suggestion to him: *he wanted the engineer to allow some of his prisoners to escape!* Finally Giskes convinced the civilian that these escapees would be helping the German cause. Now Giskes told the engineer of his plan. The engineer, who came from Saxony (once a hotbed of anti-Nazism in the early thirties, especially in the great industrial towns of the area), should pose as a secret Communist. Everywhere, as Giskes knew, Communist cells were springing up again in Germany, now it was clear that the country was almost defeated. Both the Americans and Russians were parachuting in agents to help spread the influence of these German Communists. He would approach certain selected 'booty Germans', explain to them his true sympathies, and ask them if they would carry messages from him to the Americans on the other side of the border if he could manage to help them to escape.

The engineer agreed, and the great scheme commenced. By now Giskes had dreamed up his own great counter-attack. Surprisingly enough it was quite close to the 'small solution', as those German generals who opposed Hitler's plan and had suggested another, more modest scheme of their own, called it. It envisaged a two-pronged German attack on the border city of Aachen.

Recently captured by the Americans, the old imperial city had prestige and strategic value; for in addition to being Charlemagne's own city from which he had ruled his great empire in the eighth century, it posed a threat to the Rhineland and the road to Cologne.

The 'Giskes Plan', the two-pronged attack on the American held city from the direction of Cologne fitted in exactly with the predictions of most Allied intelligence chiefs; for such an offensive would explain the presence (or so they believed) of Sepp Dietrich's missing Sixth SS Panzer Army in that general area.

Now the first of the 'escapees' was aided by the engineer. With him, as he 'broke out' of the camp one dark night in November, he carried a rough sketch of the 'Giskes Plan' and other 'secret details' written on scraps of paper in milk. These were hidden in the lining of an old tobacco pouch which the escapee was instructed to hand over to the first American officer he met on reaching the American lines. He was instructed, too, to tell the Americans that if they wanted more information smuggled to them by similar means, they should include the words 'And regards to Otto from Saxony', the supposed Communist engineer, in the next daily news in

German beamed into the Reich by Radio Luxembourg, the one-time commercial radio station now being used for propaganda and espionage purposes by the Americans.

Ten days after the first 'slave labourer', as they invariably called themselves later after Allied victory, escaped, it gave Giskes in his HQ just south of Bonn a certain amount of sardonic pleasure to hear the announcer from Radio Luxembourg say, among the flood of personal messages to Germany, 'And tonight we send regards to Otto from Saxony'.

His trick had worked! Thereafter Giskes, implementing the old techniques he had learned during those two glorious years when he had run 'North Pole' in Holland, enabled ten more Belgians and Luxembourgers to 'escape' and slip through 'enemy lines' to reach the Americans, bringing with them further information about the 'spoiling attack' to be launched near Aachen, the capture of which would be a 'Christmas present for the Führer'.

Forty years later it is not known just how much Giskes' deception helped to form Allied intelligence's appreciation of German strategy in December 1944. We do know that, due to the failure of Ultra to supply anything of importance, Allied intelligence had to fall back on agents and refugees from Germany who had somehow slipped across the frontier, for their information on what was going on opposite their troops on the Ghost front and elsewhere. The intelligence summaries of the time are full of references to 'Luxembourgers' and 'refugees or escapees from the Bitburg area';* obviously front-line intelligence officers were grabbing at the slightest bit of information.

We also know that the last two intelligence summaries issued by First Army's Chief-of-Intelligence Colonel 'Monk' Dickson stated:

> The enemy's armoured reserve appears to be quartered along the railroads, generally in a semi-circle from Düsseldorf to Coblenz with Köln as a centre point. He has brought up and continues to bring up Army and Corps artillery formations and to build up his

---

* The largest city in the future area of battle

fighter and fighter-bomber strength on the Western Front. It is plain that his strategy in defence of the Reich is based on the exhaustion of our offensive, to be followed by an all-out counter-attack with armour between the Roer and Erft.

Dickson concluded that an imminent Allied attack 'must be considered the greatest threat to the successful defence of the Reich' and that von Rundstedt would 'make good the Siegfried Line, *recapture the forts lost in the Aachen area*, accepting defeats in the south rather than compromise his hope of a decisive success in the north' (my italics).

Five days later, on 15 December, Dickson came out even more strongly for the attack on Aachen, stating that in his view the Germans would attack between 15 and 25 December. How seriously Colonel Dickson took his own warning and how successful Giskes had been with his Operation 'Heinrich' are evidenced by the fact that on that Friday, one day before the great German surprise attack hit First Army's Ghost front with all its massive weight, the good Colonel took himself off to Paris for a well-earned seventy-two hours leave!

Now Colonel Giskes could rest on his laurels, content that once again he had done a good job. Who else could have used the services of Allied citizens at this late stage of the war for Germany's purposes?

'By now, I knew from my travels in the Eifel that month', Giskes recalled more than three decades later at his retirement home in Rottach-Eigern, 'that something big was happening. I hoped naturally that I hadn't dreamed up the "real" counter-attack for the unsuspecting Americans, as I had warned Model's Chief-of-Intelligence I might do. All the same, the sight of so many troops, so much armour, so many new guns everywhere behind the front, made me think of March 1918* and feel a new sense of hope. Perhaps there was a chance for Germany, at this late hour, after all? So I relaxed, my operation wound up, waiting to see what would

---

* The last German offensive of World War I, which sent the British Fifth Army reeling back miles in great disorder.

happen in the Eifel, looking forward to Christmas a little, my first in Germany for several years. How little did I know then that it would be my last in the Homeland for years to come and under what circumstances I could be spending next Christmas . . . behind Swedish curtains,* almost without hope!'

So Giskes rested, his work done, the Allies in the Ardennes successfully fooled about German intentions. Now it was up to the fighting men, the young men eager for some desperate glory and the chance to die for 'Folk, Fatherland and Führer'.

4

On the morning of 9 December Colonel Baron von der Heydte started to receive the first of the drafts promised him the day before by General Student. As he had already guessed, the élite of the four parachute divisions under Student's command in Holland turned out to be the usual dead-beats and trouble-makers that battalion commanders normally manage to post off to other commanders on such occasions. As the Baron commented later, 'Never during my entire fighting career had I been in command of a unit with less fighting spirit.' But then who gives up his best soldiers to another unit?'

That day, as his staff worked feverishly to put the 1,200-strong unit together for a supposed jump on the Eastern front, von der Heydte discovered that only 200 to 300 of his paras were veterans who had taken part with him in the last operational jump in Crete three long years before; the rest had never jumped in combat before. He was heartened a little, however, to find that of those with combat experience 150 had somehow dodged the decision by Student and sneaked from his own unit to join him. They were a welcome sight that December day.

---

* German slang for 'behind bars'

Hastily von der Heydte set to work to knock the hybrid unit into shape, still unaware of his mission. By the twelfth, he had formed a battle group made up of four para companies, a signals section, a section of heavy mortars and a company of engineers. Arms and equipment came flooding in. All he lacked now was the necessary jump equipment.

On the morning of 13 December, he reported to General Student, as ordered, that his unit was ready, apart from the parachutes – and a mission! The parachutes were speedily supplied to his next camp. But as far as the mission was concerned, all that Student could, or would, tell him was that his combat unit was now under the command of Air Fleet West, attached, surprisingly enough, to Sepp Dietrich's Sixth SS Panzer Army. And that was that.

Late that day, von der Heydte and his men were ordered to report to the great German training camp, dating from the days of the Kaiser, at Sennelager; he would receive further instructions there. Immediately, von der Heydte set off with the advance party, leaving his men to follow by convoy, on the long trek down blacked-out roads for northern Germany where once he had served with the 15th Cavalry at Paderborn, the nearest town to the camp.

Confusion reigned when he arrived there late at night. No one expected him. The harassed camp commandant told the perplexed and not a little annoyed colonel that he had received no orders to accommodate a new force of 1,200 men. A weary von der Heydte called the Chief-of-Staff at the headquarters of the nearby Münster Air Region. There, they knew nothing about parachutists, either, or the airfields from which they were supposed to fly; the one von der Heydte had mentioned was not even built yet! The Chief-of-Staff, therefore, refused to find von der Heydte accommodation for the night, snorting, 'If this sort of thing goes on, anybody could turn up! *Ends!*' With that he slammed down the phone, leaving von der Heydte speechless.

Other telephone calls for help proved equally frustrating and purposeless, and something else made von der Heydte uneasy. The camp was packed with the SS troopers of the Parachute Corps' *bête noire*, Obersturmbannführer Otto Skorzeny. Obviously they too were scheduled to take part in

this mysterious mission; and von der Heydte, who regarded
Skorzeny as a Viennese upstart who had stolen the kudos of
rescuing Mussolini from his mountain-top prison the year
before from under the noses of the Parachute Corps,* didn't
like that one bit.

In the end von der Heydte had a brain-wave. He remembered a former comrade of the 15th Cavalry, a reserve officer
who now functioned as a chemist in the nearby village of
Oerlinghausen. Von der Heydte called him. Flattered to be
addressed as 'my dear fellow' by the 'Hero of Crete', the
chemist said he'd take care of the matter immediately. And he
did. As von der Heydte commented later, 'Something which
the Camp Commandant of Sennelager and the Chief of the
Air Staff could not do was taken care of within the hour by a
village chemist!' At four o'clock in the morning, as the first
of von der Heydte's trucks began to roll into the dreamy
little medieval village, the chemist had aroused every householder and arranged for billets for the weary men. By
dawn on 14 December, his 1,200 men were fast asleep. But
even as von der Heydte finally closed his eyes after a long
and frustrating day, two basic questions still remained un-
answered: where and how was the operation going to take
place?

At midday he received his first enlightenment. A familiar face
appeared around the door of the chemist's house in which he
had set up his headquarters. It was the face of a man he had
not seen since May 1941 when he had made his combat jump
into Crete. It was Major Erdmann of the Luftwaffe.

Now Erdmann was in command of the so-called 'Stalingrad
Squadron', the unit that had supplied von Paulus's army
trapped at Stalingrad in the winter of 1942–43. For a while
the old comrades chatted, then Erdmann broached the subject of his presence in Oerlinghausen. He had been informed
that he was to use his 120 Junkers 52s, that venerable three-

---

*The Mussolini rescue had been nominally under the command of
General Student, and his men took part in the actual rescue. Spontaneous-
ly, however, Skorzeny, who had led the rescue attack, jumped into
Mussolini's plane after he had been freed and flew with him to Vienna.

engined transport plane known as 'Auntie Ju' by its crews, in a practice jump by von der Heydte's paras.

Von der Heydte soon informed Erdmann that this was no practice. He had been ordered to prepare for a combat jump. Erdmann was horrified. He was the sole survivor of the original 'Stalingrad Squadron'. All the experienced crews had either been killed or posted elsewhere. His pilots were 'green-beaks' the lot of them, direct from the training schools, who had never done any night flying and had never dropped paratroops operationally. His crews could *not* drop paras operationally.

In dismay the two of them drove to see the Commander-in-Chief Air Fleet West that afternoon, arriving at his head-quarters near Diez in the Taunus Forest late that evening. The Air Force general seemed more interested in his bottle of brandy than their problems.

Here for the first time von der Heydte learned his mission. His battle group, attached to Dietrich's Sixth SS Army, was to be dropped by Erdmann's squadron in front of the SS Panzers to open up the way for them.

Erdmann protested that his unit was not ready.

The General did not seem interested. At all events he gave no reply. So Erdmann asked, 'How will the co-operation with the Luftwaffe be executed, sir?'

Carelessly the General waved his cognac glass in the air. 'You'd better go and see General Pelz. He'll know about that.' Thereupon the two officers were dismissed, and drove furiously through the night to find Pelz, the commander of the Tactical Air Force in the Eifel. He knew nothing, either. So they set off again, speeding dangerously down blacked-out, icy country roads, being stopped periodically by hard-eyed suspicious military policemen until finally, in the early hours of the morning of 14 December, they reached Field Marshal Model's HQ at Münstereifel.

It was three o'clock in the morning, but General Krebs, Model's Chief-of-Staff, was still awake, as were most of the officers in the Army HQ, still working furiously to iron out the final difficulties. He received the Colonel and Major almost at once and filled them in on the details of the great new attack to be launched out of the Eifel in exactly forty-eight hours' time.

Von der Heydte's men were to be dropped between Eupen and Malmédy on the heights above the former town, which was the headquarters of the American General Gerow's Fifth Corps. Once Dietrich's SS Panzers attacked westwards into Middleton's VIIIth Corps, it was expected that Gerow would start sending troops from the Eupen area to help his hard-pressed fellow-commander. By dominating the road network, von der Heydte would stop those Amis.

Now it was von der Heydte's turn to express his doubts about the success of his surprise mission, while Krebs listened attentively. In the end he was so impressed by what von der Heydte that he awakened his chief, Field Marshal Model. (Both Model and Krebs were to commit suicide before the war was over.)

Model, one of Hitler's most competent and aggressive commanders, was clearly 'at the end of his tether', as von der Heydte recalled much later, but he had not lost his old habits of directness and precision. After listening to von der Heydte's protests, he asked bluntly, 'Do you give your parachute drop ten per-cent chance of success?'

'*Jawohl*', the Baron replied dutifully, 'between ten and twenty per-cent.'

'Lucky fellow,' Model said grimly. 'I wish the whole offensive had the same kind of chance. Then it is necessary to make the attempt, since the entire offensive is the last remaining chance we have of concluding the war favourably. If we don't make the most of that ten per-cent chance, Germany will be faced by certain defeat.'

Baron von der Heydte gave way to the unassailable logic of the little Field Marshal's words. Together with Erdmann, he set off yet again to find the headquarters of the Sixth SS Panzer Army, fighting the crowded roads and the fog which was drifting in from the fir woods everywhere.

Sepp Dietrich was already up by the time von der Heydte reached it – and already obviously slightly drunk. Dietrich, a Bavarian like the Baron, was a completely different person from the kind of general officer the latter was used to dealing with. Ex-World War I sergeant in the first German tank regiment, he had become a Party bully-boy and risen to command the *Leibstandarte Adolf Hitler*, the Ist SS Division, by the start of the war. From that post he had worked himself up, through corps commander, until now he commanded some eight divisions or more, four of them the best armoured divisions that Germany still possessed. 'A good fellow', von Rundstedt said of him, 'but he shouldn't have been allowed to command more than a division.' Now he had been given the honour by the Führer himself of making the decisive break-through in the Ardennes and reaching the Channel coast: an assignment which he personally thought impossible. Hence the drink in the early morning.

Almost immediately it was clear that the aristocrat and the peasant were not going to hit it off, in spite of the efforts of Dietrich's Chief-of-Staff, General Kraemer, an elegant ex-Wehrmacht officer, to mediate between the two of them. Dietrich's first question was: 'What can you paratroopers do, anyway?'

Coldly the aristocrat replied, 'Give me the mission, General, and then I can evaluate the feasibility.'

'All right,' Dietrich slapped the map with his butcher's paw (he had once been an apprentice butcher). 'Take that spot marked X on it.' He slapped the map again and again, rapping out, 'Or this one . . . or this!'

All the while the elegant Kraemer kept drumming the table with his fingers and interrupting Dietrich with angry asides, snorting, 'This is crazy. . . . What a lunatic operation!'

At last von der Heydte got a moment to study the four objectives which Dietrich apparently had assigned to him. He was not pleased with them. Looking up at the broad-faced Dietrich with his bristly moustache in the style of Hitler, he said coldly, 'I should have to have the whole division if I am to hold this area until the arrival of the armour. These objectives are also too far off.'

Dietrich didn't like it, but in the end he compromised. Von der Heydte would drop at Baraque Michel, just beyond the highest point in the whole of the Ardennes, to take the crossroads leading to Verviers, Eupen and Malmédy. The jump would take place before the great artillery bombardment commenced at 5.30 on the morning of 16 December.

'You will go there and make confusion,' Dietrich said thickly.

Hastily Kraemer interrupted his chief, and said, 'It is not von der Heydte who is to make the confusion, Obergruppen-führer. That is Skorzeny.'

Von der Heydte frowned. *Again Skorzeny!* What was going on? However, he didn't pursue the point. Instead, he asked about the kind of opposition he could expect from the Americans once he had landed.

Angrily Dietrich answered, 'I'm not a prophet! You'll learn earlier than I what forces the Americans will employ against you. Besides, behind their lines there are only Jewish hoodlums – and bank managers.'

Kraemer looked up at the ceiling in despair at his chief's assessment of the opposition, but he said nothing, as von der Heydte talked Dietrich into giving him a liaison officer armed with a radio from the 12th SS Panzer Division. But the Baron knew the radio would not be enough. In Crete, as in all paradrops, things had gone wrong, radios had got lost; he needed pigeons.

Dietrich exploded. '*Pigeons!* Don't be stupid. Pigeons! I'm leading my whole damn army without pigeons! You should be able to lead *one* battle group without a damn menagerie!'

On that unhappy note, the sole meeting between the aristocrat and the peasant ended. Von der Heydte was taken outside to be shown whatever material the Sixth had on his proposed DZ, which wasn't very much.

But now the Baron discovered the Skorzeny connection. The name given to his operation was '*Unternehmen Stoesser*' ('Auk'); that to Skorzeny's '*Unternehmen Grief*' ('Gryphon'). By chance when he asked an NCO for the papers referring to the former and they were brought to him, Baron von der Heydte discovered that the documents bore the wrong code-name.

As he wrote later, 'People clearly wanted to keep Skorzeny's mission from me. . . . Only through this NCO's mistake did I learn of Skorzeny's plan.'

He asked the staff for further details. They were 'extremely reticent'. But von der Heydte wanted nothing to do with the Viennese parvenu (and perhaps with his lawyer's eye to the future he desired not to be associated with a man who obviously was going to be in serious trouble with the Allies if they won the war – which the Baron was sure they would). Energetically he insisted that the Skorzeny operation should not interfere with his own dropping zone. In the end he convinced Dietrich's staff that they should order boundaries laid down between him and Skorzeny and that passwords should be issued to prevent confusion on the day.

That was that. He had achieved at least a minor victory over the SS. Exhausted by his days on the road chasing from one headquarters to another with so little result, the Baron and Major Erdmann commenced the long journey to Oerlinghausen and the new problems which would undoubtedly face the two of them there. Snoring in the back of the staff car, they rode off into the grey December day. Now there were exactly twenty-four hours left before the great operation commenced.

5

On the morning of Friday, 15 December, British General John Whitely, Eisenhower's Assistant Chief-of-Staff, told Allied Air Force commanders that there was nothing to report from the Ardennes sector. It was a view from the top on future activity on the Ghost front which seemed to be accepted everywhere.

Montgomery's Chief-of-Staff, Freddie de Guingand, was already on leave in England and soon his chief would follow him; for on that last Friday before the avalanche descended upon the unsuspecting Americans on the Ghost front, he wrote to Eisenhower: 'If you have no objection I would like to hop over to England on Saturday, 23 December and spend Christmas with my son. I have not seen him since D-Day.' Thereupon he flew to Eindhoven to have a round of golf with Welsh professional Dai Rees. Rank hath its privileges, even in the midst of total war!

It was no different further down the chain of command. The fact that nearly 600,000 German troops had been gathering under their very noses for the last six weeks had still not come to the attention of the generals commanding the armies at the front. On that Friday General Bradley, commanding the US Eighteenth Army Group, and General Hodges of the US First Army, were, like Montgomery, away from their commands. In their case, they were being tape-measured by a Belgian shotgun manufacturer for custom-made hunting rifles. Even Colonel 'Monk' Dickson, who later claimed to have spotted the coming offensive in the Ardennes, was on his way for his 'seventy-two hours' in Paris. Soon he and his commander Hodges would be fleeing for their lives, or so they thought, with the Germans at their very heels.

It was the same right down to the front line. At the front-line village of Honsfeld, to be overrun by waves of Germans within the next twenty-four hours, a movie was being shown at the 99th Division's rest camp. The sound track broke down, and the angry GIs delivered their own ribald dialogue as the projectionist sweated to get the camera working again. Later, as the men filed out to the recreation hut, there was a rumour that Marlene Dietrich would give the next show at the camp (later she would claim that she had been saved in the nick of time from being captured by her fellow-countrymen by a full general of American paratroops landing at her very feet).

It was no different in the lines of the US 14th Cavalry, soon too to be overrun by the Germans. Many of the men who would be dead, captured or running for their lives the next morning, this night watched a USO show, including a male singer who sang and ate crackers at the same time. But then the quality of front-line USO shows wasn't the best.

Beyond the 14th Cavalry's sector of the front, at that of the ill-fated 106th US Infantry Division, which would soon suffer the worst defeat of any US division in the European theatre of operations, the situation was little different. That day there were no USO shows for the 106th, for they had not yet set up their rest camps and all the rest of the long organisational tail, of which the riflemen said cynically, 'Yeah, one man in the line and five men to bring up the Coca-Cola!' For the 106th had been in the line exactly four days now, and they were too busy trying to find their way and keep warm in the freezing hcights of the Eifel-Ardennes. All the same the men of the 106th, who would soon suffer a staggering 10,000 casualties in killed, wounded and prisoners, had no idea that the Germans would attack them in such force. Hadn't the veterans of the 2nd Infantry Division called as they had vacated their positions to the 106th, 'Lucky guys, you're coming to a rest camp!' And that day nineteen-year-old Pfc Joe Schectman was writing to his parents in the States, 'Never expected your little boy to get this far, did you. We are billeted as comfortably and as safely as we were in England. . . . Of course, there is no telling how long I'll be in this paradise. But as long as I am, I'll be safe.'

The veteran 28th US Division, which had been badly hit in the fighting of Hürtgen Forest the previous month, too, rested in its positions that Friday, unaware that soon it would be attacked in overwhelming strength. Its 110th Regiment, packed with reinforcements, which would soon be virtually destroyed, was too concerned with licking them into shape to be worried by the Germans.

Its commander, Colonel Hurley Fuller, rough-tongued and abrasive, had been fired from his last regiment because of his inability to curb his temper. Now he had the 110th Regiment and he knew that it was his last chance to make good. He had fought in World War I and was well into middle age. If he wanted to 'make general', the dream of all Regular Army officers, he had to transform the battered regiment back into an effective fighting force once more. As far as he was concerned, what the Germans were up to on the snowy heights on the other side of the River Our was no concern of his at the moment. However, he'd soon learn differently – and he would never 'make general' because of it.

All seemed so quiet and innocent along the whole length of the Ghost front on the last day of the three months of peace which had reigned in that remote hilly, wooded area. Next in line to the 28th Division, the last of the American units to be so savagely attacked on the morrow, the 4th Infantry Division recorded in its official journal that their G-2 left for a three-day pass to 'civilazation' (*sic*). How far that unnamed staff officer ever got on his way to the flesh-pots in the rear has

never been detailed. Perhaps he didn't make it. For by the
time that the storm which was soon to sweep over the Ghost
front in all its terrifying, lethal fury abated, there would be
thousands, many thousands, of young Americans who never
again would see that 'civilazation'.

On the other side of the line that snowy, cold Friday, the
young Germans of the attack formations waited too; and with
them the men of half-a-dozen clandestine organisations who
had made the surprise attack possible, or who would lead it in
its various manifestations.

At Oerlinghausen, far to the rear, von der Heydte's paras
at last accepted delivery of their chutes. They were something
completely new to them: captured Russian parachutes,
triangular in shape without the usual parachute vent at
the top. Apparently its design was calculated to reduce the
usual oscillation which took place during a drop so that
the para would have little difficulty in controlling his
chute. It was a design for which von der Heydte was duly
grateful; it might help his untrained youngsters to jump
more safely and not be swept away from the main body of
veterans.

That Friday von der Heydte had received another little gift:
straw dummies attached to worn-out, old-fashioned parachutes, 300 of them in all. The dropping of these dummies was
no new trick, the Baron knew. Back on the day of the invasion
the Allies had dropped them between Rouen and Le Havre to
make the German defenders, of which one was von der
Heydte himself, believe an attempt was being made to
capture the Seine crossings. Now these dummies were
to be launched from aircraft not far from his own DZ to mis-
lead the Americans as to the correct location of the dropping zone. Again von der Heydte was pleased. Every little
helped.

Now he and his men waited, the parachutists' chins buried
in their double-padded chin straps, thick rubber rings around
their knees, ankles tightly bandaged, weighed down with
almost 100 pounds of equipment per man.

Skorzeny's men were in their concentration areas too, just
behind the front in the Sixth SS Panzer Army's area. For six

days his Panzerbrigade 150 had taken circuitous routes, moving only at night, until they had reached the forests between Münstereifel and Stadtkyll. Now it was hiding there, protected from prying eyes by the feared Gestapo itself. As soon as Kampfgruppe* Peiper of the 1st SS Panzer Division, commanded by the dashing young 29-year-old Colonel Jochen Peiper, had broken through the Ami front at Losheim, Skorzeny's 'Americans' would take advantage of the confusion and panic to grab one of the vital bridges across the River Meuse for the 1st SS.

Now Skorzeny waited with his Brigade, his headquarters set up in two rooms in a little dwelling house at the edge of the Eifel township at Schmidtheim. There would be no sleep for him this night for he, too, felt the tension just as did, in his words, 'every soldier along the whole front from general to the last grenadier'.

With him he had three of his nine teams from Captain Stielau's special unit. The rest were scattered elsewhere, waiting for the signal to go. They would pretend to be members of the 5th US Armoured Division, and already they were well versed for their role, with the letters 'CD', 'XY' or 'Z' painted on the near side of the bonnet of their jeeps so that they could be recognised as Germans by German front-line units. Also each man wore a pink or blue scarf, kept the second button of his 'Ike jacket' open and would give two taps on his helmet for recognition purposes. On their way to the River Meuse, they would paint white spots on trees, houses and roads to indicate the safe routes.

But they bore more than white paint with them. Four teams carried a fortune in Belgian and French francs – namely, 30 millions' worth in brand-new notes (all forged by forced labourers inside concentration camps) to bribe Allied nationals of Skorzeny's 'sleeper organisation' left behind the previous September when the Germans had fled. It was planned that these agents would use the money to pay Communist French and Belgian harbour and rail workers a full week's money to stay away from their jobs in the week leading up to Christmas. This, it was thought, would effec-

---

* Battle group

tively sabotage the British supply system using the port of Antwerp.*

Across the border in American-held territory, there were agents too, waiting for the order to commence their activities. From Lanzerath in the north in the area of the 99th US Division to the south at Walferdingen, opposite the 24th Division, there were German observers, mostly members of the Gestapo, watching the unsuspecting Amis. At the latter place, the former Gestapo representative had simply crossed the frontier and reoccupied his own room with the key he had taken with him when he had fled the previous September. Now he was using his room as an observation post, checking the movements of American convoys as they used the main Luxembourg–Echternach road.

Deeper into Belgium, there were agents already in business at Bastogne, one of the key road crossroads high on the list of German priorities, soon to be the site of the heroic defence by the 'Battered bastards of Bastogne', the 101st US Airborne Division. That night the locals in the villages around the town which housed General Middleton's VIIIth Corps head-quarters, reported seeing signal lights and para-flares dropping into their fields.

Even further afield, the preparations for the great clan-destine operations had reached their final phase. In selected prisoner-of-war camps in Belgium, France, and even as far as England, groups of fanatical Nazi prisoners, who were in contact with the Reich, were ready to riot and if possible to break out in order to add to the confusion in the Allied rear areas.†

In the trapped German garrisons of Lorient and St Nazaire, surrounded and cut off from Germany since the previous

---

*All autumn the British had been trying to disarm the 70,000-strong Belgian partisan movement, mainly Communist, which was well armed. In November the British had quietly surrounded Brussels with an armoured division to prevent an armed Communist rising. In addition, in December 1944 British troops were also actively fighting Greek Communists in Athens.

† In the UK, one prisoner who supposedly betrayed the plot to the British was executed after sentence of death had been passed on him by a kangaroo court. His murderers were subsequently hanged.

Above. Segregated negro troops of a US field artillery batallion dig in on a Belgian highway to stand against the Nazi counter-attack.
Below Left. Obersturmbannfuehrer Jochen Peiper, C.O. 1st SS Panzer Regiment.
Right. In the shattered town of Stavelot, Belgium, the church still stands amid the ruins.

Above. Wounded German prisoners are brought in by horse-drawn sled in the US First Army sector.
Below. These soldiers of the US 28th Division were found dead in the snow. A single bullet through the head of each man and the orderly line they were laid in suggests a German atrocity was committed. Some clothes and boots had also been removed.

Above. Hitler's weather predictions were right; these German prisoners carrying a dead US soldier to an aid post have no need of a stretcher. The body was frozen solid.
Below. A formation of US C47 "Dakotas" drop much-needed supplies to the besieged American troops in Bastogne.

Above. Infantrymen of Patten's favourite regiment – the Third US Army's Fourth Armoured Division – protect the flanks as armoured vehicles move up towards besieged Bastogne. *Below*. Members of the US 101st Airborne Division – the Screaming Eagles or the Battered Bastards of Bastogne as they called themselves – finally emerge from Bastogne itself after withstanding the Nazi siege.

Above. A knocked-out Nazi tank near Bastogne.
Below. German desperation at this stage of the war was extreme. Here Nazi troops are
seen fastening their new boots as dead US soldiers lie stripped and barefoot.

Above. Alerted American troops watch overhead as vapour trails from Allied and enemy planes engaged in dog-fights.
Below. German troops pose with American cigarettes in front of an abandoned US tank destroyer.

A patrol of the US 82nd Airborne Division recount a successful operation by the light and heat of a fire in the heavy woods of the Ardennes.

Above. US complacency was all too evident from the start.
Below. German troops pass an abandoned US reconnaissance car in territory taken by their counter-offensive.

August, as well as in that only part of the British empire to come under German rule during World War II, the Channel Islands, plans were made to exploit any breakthrough in the far-off Ardennes. Under the fire-eating Admiral Huffmeier, who was in charge of the Channel Islands, a force was ready to land on the French coast and show Churchill what the men of *'Division Kanada'** could do, although they were starved and living off less than a thousand calories a day.

In the Channel, as well, coastal U-boats and E-boats waited to take advantage of the new situation, being directed to potential targets by the garrison still encircled at Dunkirk. Here it was hoped that the new surprise offensive would once again send the British fleeing from the Continent in disarray as they had done from Dunkirk in 1940. (Later, when Montgomery learned just how serious the counter-offensive was, he quipped, tongue in cheek, that there could be no 'second Dunkirk' because Dunkirk was 'still in German hands').†

Everywhere in the snow-bound countryside that fateful Friday forty years ago they waited for the order to move. The actors were in place; the drama could commence.

---

* They were so named because Canada was thought to be the destination for most of the occupiers once they had surrendered. In the end, they did carry out a landing at Granville, capture several score of surprised American soldiers and five ships, and released eighty-six German POWs. Their reward from the grateful Admiral was one teaspoonful of jam!

† On Christmas Eve, 1944, one such U-boat sank a transport carrying a whole regiment of the 66th US Division off Cherbourg. In the general confusion, the port authorities didn't even know that the ship was waiting to dock.

BOOK TWO
BLACK CHRISTMAS

Pardon my French, Lev, but just where in hell has the sonovabitch gotten all his strength?
General Bradley to General Allen, 17 December 1944

ONE

The Gryphon and the Auk

1

At one minute after midnight on Saturday, 16 December 1944, the Bletchley night shift was alerted. For weeks, with no messages of any importance coming from Germany, the staff of the cryptanalytical and processing huts had begun to believe that the war had passed them by. They were jaded, too, by the months of active, concentrated effort since D-Day.

Now, suddenly, the German High Command was transmitting again after long weeks of absolute silence. What was going on? Why had the long, silent front in Western Europe abruptly burst into activity?

Tensely the men and women of the night shift, some of them perhaps already half realising that the balloon had gone up again and dreading what was to come, waited for the decode.*

They had it at last. Hastily they grouped around the boffin, as he started to read it out in the poor light of the naked bulbs of the Nissen hut. It was from Field Marshal Gerd von Rundstedt, and it was addressed to all his field commanders, to be passed on to subordinate units. 'The hour of destiny has struck,' it stated. 'Mighty offensive armies face the Allies.

---

*There was more than one case of a person collapsing at 'Station X' because he or she was unable to stand up to the strain of yet another 'flap'.

91

Everything is at stake. More than mortal deeds are required as a holy duty to the Fatherland!'

The men and women of the night shift in that remote, peaceful establishment, so far away from the blood and thunder of the front, looked at each other in shock. What did it mean? What 'mighty offensive armies'? What was at stake? What 'mortal deeds' were required at a time when Germany was virtually beaten? What was going on at the front?

Some 400 miles away in the Eifel-Ardennes, fog drifted through the snow-heavy firs, as the young men who would be in the first wave waited in their white-camouflaged suits. In the fields on both sides of the winding, hilly roads, the artillerymen crouched over their pieces expectantly. On the roads themselves, covered still with straw to deaden all noise, the tanks were packed in lone, awesome lines. All was tense, nerve-racking expectancy.

From Monschau in the north to Echternach in the south, 60 long miles of front line, the artillery commanders rapped out their reports, 'All batteries ready to fire!'

Here and there the infantrymen and the tankers exchanged the usual nervous jokes, '*See you in America, old horse. . . . Don't drink all the firewater before I get there. . . . Wait till we get to Paris and all those sweet little French cheetahs. . . .* Everywhere young soldiers urinated in the snow-filled ditches for the umpteenth time. The nervous strain, as was customary, was beginning to tell. A few last hasty puffs at cigarettes concealed in freezing, cupped hands – and then it came, the hoarse bellow from the gun commanders, '*FEUER FREI!*'

It was exactly 5.30 on the morning of 16 December 1944. Suddenly, the complete length of the Ghost front erupted in fire and flame. The whole weight of the artillery of three armies, ranging from 16-inch railway guns to 3-inch mortars, descended upon the startled Americans of the four divisions holding the line. And as the morning stillness was ripped apart by that obscene, baleful, man-made storm, the white-clad infantry burst from the forests cheering as they came and the tanks, hundreds of them, like sinister primeval monsters searching for their prey, began to roll forward.

The great attack had started at last!

For one solid hour the great barrage continued, cutting

telephone links, destroying front-line pillboxes, smashing in foxholes, turning the American first-line positions into a smoking, churned-up lunar landscape.

Then abruptly it ceased. For a few minutes there was a stunned silence as the men in the line, the survivors, attempted to collect themselves, faces ashen, unspoken questions in their wide, wild eyes. Then at key points all along the front, searchlights stabbed the fog, aiming at the clouds, trying to reflect the light downwards.*

Awed and horrified, the American infantrymen in their shattered positions stared to their front, their faces turned an eerie, glowing white in the strange light. What – what was going on?

Then they were there! The first ghostlike figures in their white camouflaged capes advancing in a slow, ominous walk, twenty abreast, weapons carried at the high port, while behind them the first tanks began to emerge from the forest, snapping off the firs like matchwood, showering the infantry packed on their decks with snow. It was unbelievable. This was the Ghost front where nothing had happened since September. They had come here to train, not to fight. Nobody had warned them about this. *But the Krauts . . . the Krauts were attacking . . . in their thousands!*

Now an overwhelming mass of German infantry and armour swamped Bradley's four divisions, two of them new to battle and two badly mauled the previous November. Immediately, the Germans achieved a surprise equalled only by Napoleon at Waterloo. Montgomery's own intelligence summary, circulated that very morning, read: 'The enemy is at present fighting a defensive campaign on all fronts; his situation is such that he cannot stage major offensive operations. Furthermore at all costs he has to prevent the war from entering the mobile phase.' Now, in front of the Americans' eyes, the German was doing both those things; staging an offensive that was decidedly mobile!

Almost immediately the enemy force began to break

---

*This was 'Monty's Moonlight', a device copied from Montgomery's attempts to light up a battlefield at night by means of searchlights.

through everywhere, from the south near Echternach, Luxembourg, to just below Monschau in the north, in Germany. Led by the infantry, the Panzers cracked the thin crust holding the front in a dozen or more places and, as the Americans reeled back in shock and sometimes in downright panic, started to probe for the major rail- and road-heads of the Ardennes – towns such as St Vith and Bastogne, which would figure so prominently in the bitter weeks of fighting to come.

Seen from above, if any plane had been able to take off on that snowy, foggy day, it would have seemed that a thick grey finger had been poked into the khaki-coloured belly of the US army in the Ardennes, thrusting ever deeper and deeper. In that characteristically swift and articulate manner of his, the old word-smith Winston Churchill would soon adapt the old slimming slogan about fighting the 'battle of the bulge' and lend that name to the whole campaign: 'The Battle of the Bulge'.

And indeed the characterisation was very apt. For as that long, bitter day passed, the battlefield in that remote border country did start to resemble a bulge, with the Americans to south and north of the killing ground holding the flanks, while the indentation spread rapidly westwards, heading for the vital River Meuse.

To the extreme left of the Bulge that dawn, a patrol of the 99th Infantry Division, alerted by the tremendous bombardment, was now making its way cautiously to the village of Lanzerath. Unknown to the handful of green soldiers under the command of First Lieutenant Lyle Bouck, 21 years old, short, stocky and determined, they were going forward into their first, and last, action; for Lanzerath stood directly in the path of 1st SS Armoured Division, which was going to make the dash for the River Meuse.

Now as the bombardment died away in the hills to their rear, the little patrol, creeping forward down the snowy road into the white-painted village grouped round its slate-roofed church, saw the first of the tank destroyers and armoured cars of their neighbour, the 14th Cavalry, already beginning its retreat to the safety of the rear. Still they pressed on, nervous and tense, laden with ammunition; for, green as they were, they anticipated trouble this day. They would meet it in due course.

Now they entered the village. A hundred yards to their left up the single village street there was the building abandoned by the men of the 14th Cavalry. Cautiously, hugging the walls of the houses, Lieutenant Bouck's little patrol started to approach it. The place was the best observation post in the village. From it they could see right into Germany itself. Perhaps from there they could discover the meaning of that tremendous bombardment.

Lieutenant Bouck halted his patrol with a gesture of his hand. He pointed forward. Four men scrambled up and charged the house. They were taking no chances. In the lead 19-year-old Pfc James, an aggressive young soldier, slammed open the door and raced into the ground floor, heavy with the smell of animals and human sweat. It was empty, save for abandoned US equipment everywhere. He clattered up the steps to the second floor – and stopped short. A big man in civilian clothes was seated next to the window, which looked into Germany, calmly talking over the civilian telephone line! (Major Hill of Büllingen had been right after all!)

James whipped his bayonet out of its scabbard as the civilian spun round. He jammed it into the big man's belly. 'Reach!' he growled.

The man understood the tone, if not the English. His hands shot into the air.

Breathlessly Lieutenant Bouck ran into the room. James recommended that they should kill the man. He was obviously a German spy, reporting American movements back to the enemy over the other side of the frontier.

Bouck wasn't so sure. If the Germans were coming and they were captured, it wouldn't be opportune to have one very dead German spy in their positions.

'Let him go!' he ordered.

Reluctantly, James – who would be badly wounded and a prisoner before that day was out (as would be Bouck) – jerked his bayonet at the big civilian, and cried, 'Okay, beat it!'

The German did not need a second invitation. With a big grin he vanished down the stairs. A moment later he was running down the village street, heading for the Reich. An hour later German paratroopers were swarming everywhere through the fields towards the little platoon. By nightfall all eighteen of the men of that platoon would be dead, wounded or captured, thanks to that German infiltrator and scores like them, who were now slipping through the American lines everywhere, preparing the way for the great dash to the River Meuse.

Five miles south of where Lieutenant Bouck and his young men were soon to fight their first and last battle, Heinz Rohde, the signals NCO who had wanted a cushy billet, now alias Sergeant Morris Woodahl of the US army, found himself driving with his companions through a deserted wood. 'While the jeep bounced up and down like a young, frisky deer', he recalled after the war, 'the jeep team carried out a crazy striptease, getting rid of the para-overalls to reveal the US uniforms beneath.' 'The first burning American truck loomed up. Hurriedly we put on the American helmets. Not a second too soon. A group of Amis appeared out of the trees, dragging up an anti-tank gun. It was comforting to see that, apart from the mud that covered our uniforms, there was no difference between them and us.'

A sergeant tried to stop them. Couldn't they give a hand with the cannon? The Germans were coming! They cried back that they couldn't stop; they had orders. They burst out of the forest and on to a country road. Suddenly their hearts almost stopped beating. 'An Ami, as tall as a tree, was standing there, and there was no missing the white stripes of the military policeman around his helmet!'

But the MP was only trying to help them. He waved them on to a side trail just as German artillery shells started to fall on the road they were taking. On two wheels the jeep driver whipped round the curve on the trail and out of danger, as their own shells ploughed up the earth on both sides of the little vehicle.

'Naturally we thought at first that every Ami could spot us as Germans from a thousand metres away. But the shelling, the poor light, and the confusion of the opposition helped us through those first tense hours. Slowly we began to realise that our disguises were working and gradually our nerves started to settle down.'

Little did they know how weak their cover was, for it was 'only weeks later that we realised that an Ami jeep was normally manned by only two, at the most three men, *never four!*'

Steadily the four men of the Stielau Unit rolled westwards. Snow had begun to fall. A white carpet started to cover the fields on both sides of the narrow Belgian country roads. Now it was almost midday, and they had been driving well behind the US lines for nearly six hours. They decided to make a break. Carefully they drove the jeep into a fire break in the woods and camouflaged it. They consulted their maps and discovered to their joy that they were right on target: they were just off the main road which led to their objective, the bridge across the River Meuse at the Belgian town of Huy. They set up their radio, crouching there in the snow-bound wood, and started to send a high-speed message back to Obersturmbannführer Skorzeny, far off on the other side of the border. The way for the long-range reconnaissance to the Meuse was open.

It was then that Rohde's team received their greatest shock of the first day of their bold mission. Just as the operator was about to close down his set, there came the crackle of another voice acknowledging their message – *in English!*

'Who could describe our surprise and joy, as some unknown Ami operator acknowledged receipt at the top of his voice!' Now confident that they would succeed, they mounted up again and began to roll along the packed road which led to Huy and the key bridge.

While the long-range teams tried to penetrate the American rear areas on their way towards the Meuse, the short-range jeep teams carried out a far more dangerous mission directly in the front line or just behind it. It was their job to sabotage, reconnoitre and confuse, and they did it to perfection that first morning of the great surprise attack.

Almost immediately one of the teams notched up a great success. Thanks to the efforts of agents in northern France and eastern Belgium, the Germans already knew the details of the land lines linking the various major US headquarters. Now one team found and cut the direct line between Hodges' First Army HQ at Spa and Bradley's Eighteenth Army Group at Namur. Thus, for hours that were crucial, as the German armoured troops prepared to blast a hole deep into the heart of Hodges' First Army, Courtney Hodges was cut off from his superior commander, who alone could send him the assistance he would soon vitally need if he were to stop the Germans.

Another jeep team penetrated the biggest town to the front of the Sixth SS Panzer Army and reported that the Amis were fleeing; the town of Malmédy was wide open, apart from a few engineers engaged in second-line maintenance operations. Somehow or other, the Americans picked up that same message later and believed it. As a result, Malmédy was to be bombed three times by planes of what the bitter American troops located there would call 'the American Luftwaffe' (the US Ninth Air Force) with several hundred Belgian and American casualties.

One jeep team was bold enough to post itself at a vital crossroads and act as MPs. In the end it succeeded in directing down the wrong road a whole American regiment hurrying to the front as reinforcements!

Another team reported US troops massing in the Liège area. Yet another located fuel dumps on the route to be taken by Dietrich's Panzers, which were critically short of fuel and would have to rely on American supplies to carry them beyond the Meuse. According to later reports, probably highly exaggerated, the Skorzeny jeep teams were here, there and everywhere that Saturday, sabotaging and confusing and relaying back vital information to Dietrich's Sixth SS Panzer Army.

As yet the spy fever which would grip the whole of Western Europe, thanks to Skorzeny, had not yet made its appearance, in spite of the fact that one of his teams had been discovered for what they were.

Near the township of Poteau, close to the front-line city of St Vith, a group of 'American soldiers' appeared that day riding on a self-propelled gun. It was one abandoned by the fleeing men of the 14th Cavalry. A sergeant saw them pass and thought that the boots of these 'American soldiers' looked suspicious. Before he could challenge them, one of them shouted down, 'We're E Company!'

The sergeant reacted immediately. In the cavalry you didn't talk about 'companies'; you talked about 'squadrons' and 'troops'. He and his men opened fire immediately. The 'Americans' died instantly, taking their secrets with them. The second Stielau team to be challenged wouldn't die so quickly; and in the manner of their capture they would trigger off a panic the like of which Europe had not known since May 1940. But that was still to come.

2

The first close-range jeep team from Captain Stielau's clandestine unit made its first report to Skorzeny just after noon, roughly at the same time that Rohde reported in from the road to Huy. But in spite of their excellent news, Otto Skorzeny was an unhappy man. By this time he should have been across the border right behind Jochen Peiper, ready to exploit the breakthrough and race for the Meuse with his Brigade.

Instead, he found himself in a monstrous track-jam that stretched right from Belgium into Germany. At Losheim, where he had hoped to cross after Peiper, Skorzeny found a helpless confusion of tanks, trucks, heavy bridging equipment, supply vehicles, even horse-drawn artillery, mingled with stalled German infantry and hundreds of the Ami prisoners squelching miserably through the slush and mud to the rear.

Apparently, further up on the heights to his front where Lieutenant Bouck and his men, as well as other desperate American soldiers from half-a-dozen outfits, were fighting their last battles, the infantry of the 3rd German Parachute Division had bogged down. As a consequence, Peiper had not been able to advance with his battle group. In a rage he had taken the point of his 1st SS personally. He was to be committed at midnight, and by then he wanted to be at his starting line, which was on the heights to his front, now shrouded in thick brown smoke, broken now and again by the cherry-red flame of a shell exploding.

Tough, ruthless veteran of the bitter fighting in Russia, Peiper ordered his half-tracks to push through the horse-drawn artillery of a People's Division clogging his road. They did so, cutting down mercilessly anything which stood in their way. But not for long. Suddenly, the lead half-track rose into the air, violent flame erupting beneath it. Next moment it slammed down on to the road again, one track sprawling behind it like a broken limb. '*Minen . . . Ami Minen!*' someone bellowed to the rear hoarsely.

But Peiper was not to be stopped. He ordered the next half-track up to clear the crippled vehicle out of the way and carry on. But it was not to be that easy. Five minutes later, the second half-track ran over a mine too, and came to an abrupt halt. By the time he had reached the end of the dead straight road from Losheim, Peiper had lost six half-tracks, with the traffic clogging up more densely than ever behind him.

At Losheim Skorzeny, watching all this, felt a sense of despair. He could see that some of the men of his outfit were no longer convinced of success for their bold dash for the Meuse. Others were still full of enthusiasm. From the latter he picked three teams, mostly sailors, who were now to set off, spreading the word among the Americans still holding out on the ridgeline that the Germans were coming. He hoped that they would also be able to find an alternative route out of the present hopeless bottle-neck so that his brigade could advance with Peiper. That done, he set off to the headquarters of the 1st SS Corps to report his findings. His mood was mixed, for it had been a morning of successes and disappointments. It was clear that his teams were fully successful; they were fooling the Amis all right; but it was always obvious that Panzerbrigade 150 would not be moving out this day. He made up his mind. He would ask Corps to allow him to postpone his great Trojan Horse operation to the morrow. It was only later, much later, that he was to realise that the way to the Meuse – beyond that thin crust still holding out in the border villages of Belgium – was wide open. But, by then, Germany had virtually lost the battle.

Baron von der Heydte had suffered a similarly frustrating morning. Ever since the previous night, his paras, dressed and ready for action, had been waiting for transport to take them to the airfield. But as in all armies, there had been the normal bureaucratic mess and mix-up. Officially Germany's para-troops came under the jurisdiction of the Luftwaffe, although for years they had been fighting as ground troops under the command of the army. Since they were supplied by the air force, it was up to that organisation to provide them with the petrol to transport the paras to the airfield. But the air force maintained that it had been their task only to transport the paras as far as Oerlinghausen; thereafter the army was re-sponsible for petrol. Confused, angry, hardly able to believe that such things could happen in a ruthless, totalitarian system such as that of the Third Reich, von der Heydte pulled out the stops, telephoning anyone he could think of in authority in order to obtain the precious petrol.

But it was the same as it had been four days before when he and his men had first moved north to Oerlinghausen–Sennelager. Nobody wanted to take responsibility for this hybrid outfit, that was supplied by the Luftwaffe but fought for the Wehrmacht. All he received after hours of argu-ment was enough petrol to move 400 men to the airfield – and a visit from an officer from the German Judge-Advocate's branch.

Almost immediately he began cross-examining von der Heydte and his officers for the reason for delay, as if they were suspects – and in the German army it was not wise to be suspected of disloyalty or cowardice in the winter of 1944. A firing squad or a noose thrown over the nearest lamp post might well be the outcome.

In the end, von der Heydte, the former graduate student of international law, managed to convince the Kriegsrichter that the delay was not his fault. Finally the required petrol began to arrive to take the weary men to their fields at Paderborn and Lippspringe. An exhausted von der Heydte thought he'd grab a few hours sleep before the Junkers took off. But that wasn't to be. Just then Kraemer, Dietrich's Chief-of-Staff, rang up.

He told von der Heydte, 'The offensive has not progressed as rapidly as expected in our sector.'

The Baron waited. Had his ill-fated para-drop been cancelled after all? He hoped so.

But General Kraemer disappointed him. He went on to say, 'We have reached only a very small portion of our objectives. The enemy is still resisting forward of Elsenborn Camp in anticipation of reinforcements arriving from the north.'

Then it came,

'You will, therefore, drop before dawn tomorrow morning in the area previously agreed with the object of intercepting those reinforcements. Hold on as long as possible.' There was a note of pleading in the elegant, cynical Chief-of-Staff's voice now. 'Two days as a minimum – and do as much damage as you can to the reinforcements. . . . By the way, your dropping zone has been moved slightly south-eastwards to the Belle-Croix crossroads near the Baraque-Michel.'

With that Kraemer rang off, leaving the Baron more despondent than ever. A night drop was bad enough with his bunch of inexperienced youths, jumping into unknown territory, of which he knew only that it was high and marshy. Now he was to land there with light weapons, the only ones paras could carry with them, and hold out against enemy armour; for he was sure that is what the enemy would rush as reinforcements to meet the threat posed by Dietrich's Panzers, for *two whole days*! It was a tall order, a very tall order indeed. But there was no turning back. For better or worse the mission was on. Good Catholic that he was, Baron von der Heydte telephoned the local priest. Would he come out and bless the 'Auntie JUs' and their crews before they took off? He would.

Von der Heydte gave a little sigh of relief. This coming night he would need all the support he could obtain. Perhaps God might show a little mercy on his rag-tag force, flown to battle by pilots as callow and as inexperienced as they were, to hold that remote, unknown crossroads against the might of the American army?

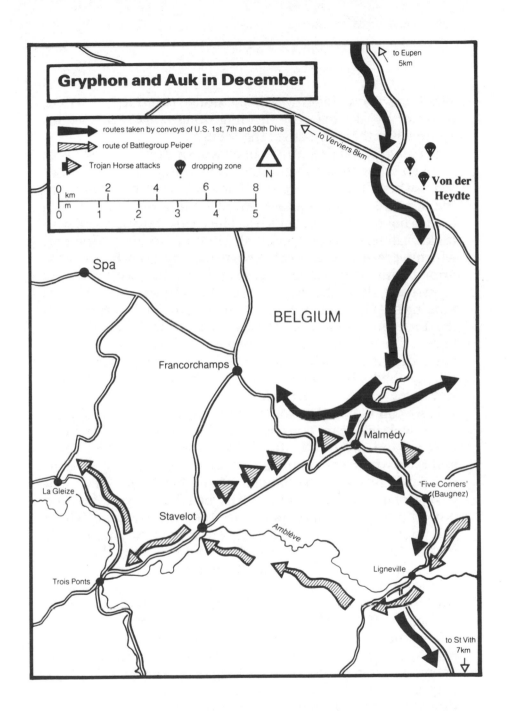

3

While the two colonels, their missions postponed, worried, plagued by doubts, the leading long-range jeep teams approached their objective, the Meuse.

Sergeant Rohde's jeep had been working its way westwards through ever-thickening American traffic all afternoon. Everywhere, the Americans, reeling back under the impact of the surprise German attack, were pulling out, taking with them a huge number of vehicles. The roads were jammed with tanks, artillery pieces, trucks, all kinds of mobile equipment, which were halted at every crossroads by grim-faced MPs, armed with walkie-talkies to keep in contact with the next crossroads along the way. As yet the 'snowdrops' were not looking for German infiltrators but American deserters from the line. For already what was soon to be called the 'big bug-out' was beginning all along the Ghost front, and the cowards, the ones whose nerve had gone, the soldiers whose officers had abandoned them 'to check with rear' were streaming westwards in panic.

It was an ideal cover for the four Germans. Yet it slowed down Rohde's team considerably. They had hoped to be at Huy around two in the afternoon. Now it was almost dark, and everywhere the American drivers were switching on their full headlights with no thought of the blackout. That sight gave Rohde's driver a shock. His headlights were blacked out, with only two slits kept free for the light to escape! There was no stopping in the tightly packed column. So, pretending that he had some sort of trouble with his motor, the driver pushed the jeep right over into the verge.

Hastily the Germans ripped open the bonnet and started working on the engine, while the driver, covered by the rest, wrenched off the blackout covers from the lights.

They had just slapped the hood down again when it happened, as, later, Rohde related: 'A jeep rolled to a stop behind us. A captain raised his long legs over the side of the jeep and came towards us. In a deep voice he asked if he should tow us to the next [motor transport] outfit.'

Behind Rohde, the driver scrambled madly into his seat

and turned the key. The jeep's motor burst into life at once. Rohde swallowed hard, glad of the growing gloom. He thanked the captain for his offer and hurried back to the jeep. One minute later they had slipped back into the long, slow column of mud-splattered, khaki-coloured vehicles and were rolling westwards once more, wondering how the other teams were getting on with their blacked-out headlights. Would they notice in time before it was too late?

At five-thirty that afternoon, Rohde's team in their jeep began to crawl slowly down the hill which led into the city of Huy. Everywhere there were American vehicles, and all thought of finding a discreet billet for the night there vanished. They reached the eastern bank of the Meuse, and not knowing exactly what to do next, except that they had to be off the streets soon (for it was pitch-black and would soon be curfew time), they began to crawl along the bank of the river, looking for a place to camp for the night.

They found it after a short while, a stretch of grassland right on the river, protected by a hedge of some kind. Hastily, they drove in and turned off engine and lights.

'Suddenly,' Rohde recalled after the war, 'there was an eerie silence, broken only by the sound of the American convoys rolling westwards and the faint boom of the guns at the front.' But the Germans had no time to pay attention to the strangeness of their surroundings, deep in the heart of the enemy camp. They had a job of work to do.

Swiftly, while the rest stood guard, weapons clutched tensely, staring hard into the icy darkness, the radio operator contacted base and relayed their vital message. They had reached the Meuse. What now?

They were told to approach the bridge over the Meuse and observe it, then to report back immediately. Their information was needed urgently at Dietrich's HQ, for so far they were the first long-range team to have reached the river.

The four Germans seized a quick meal from their supply of tinned American rations, then, leaving the driver behind to guard the jeep, they set off on their mission. Cautiously they approached the nineteenth century stone bridge, surrounded on both sides by the houses of Huy crowded up the steep banks of the Meuse, until they were about 300 yards away from it.

In spite of the blackout elsewhere and the darkness, they could see the bridge itself quite clearly, for it was outlined by the headlights of the convoys which rolled across it without ceasing. Reasoning that *they* couldn't be seen, however, the three Germans crawled ever closer, using the bank to do so, until they were within a stone's throw of the key bridge, which Peiper must cross if Dietrich's Sixth were to reach Antwerp. Unknown to the three men, shivering with fear and cold, as they crouched there, listening to the bridge vibrate with the noise of the US vehicles, Kraemer had pleaded with the young SS Colonel only hours before, 'One tank, Peiper, on that bridge . . . that's all I am asking of you. *One tank – and your mission is completed!*'

Now, in the light of the vehicles, the observers could see that the Huy Bridge was guarded. 'There were a number of typical American tents on the east bank,' Rohde recalled after the war, 'from which soldiers came and went all the time. Obviously they belonged to a guard company responsible for the bridge. Now we could see, too, the Americans positioning a searchlight on the other side of the bridge. Had they got wind of our mission?'

The three of them didn't wait to find out. As the searchlight abruptly poked a finger of icy-white light into the darkness, they doubled back to their jeep to make their report.

Swiftly they gave their impressions of the bridge, and with their nerve beginning to go after a long day behind enemy lines they begged for permission to return to their own positions. It was given. They had carried out their task well. Now Dietrich knew the kind of opposition to expect at Huy Bridge: a company of infantry armed with hand weapons, with no anti-tank cannon or flak in place. It was the kind of position that Peiper and Skorzeny had taken in *coups de main* many a time. Now it was up to the young SS Colonel to make his breakthrough in the Ardennes so that Skorzeny's 'Americans' of the 150th could rush the bridge.

But where was Jochen Peiper?

4

Just before midnight, the door of the Café Palm in the little
village of Lanzerath was flung open imperiously. Framed in
the yellow light that streamed out from the bar stood a young,
vulpine-faced officer, his cap with the silver death's head of
the Waffen SS set at a rakish angle, a look of contempt on his
tough, hard features at what he saw inside. Inside, the place
was crowded with German paras and captured Amis, one of
them wounded in the leg holding another who had lost part of
his face. Unknown to him they were Lieutenant Bouck and
Pfc James. Most of the men were fast asleep. At that moment
as the first of his Tigers started to tumble into Lanzerath, it
seemed to Obersturmbannführer Jochen Peiper that the
'front had gone to sleep'.

Pushing his way through the mob on the floor, Peiper held
up his map against the wall and stabbed it in place with the aid
of bayonets; then he turned to the commander of the 9th
Parachute Regiment, whose job it had been this long, frustrating December day to break through and clear a path for
Peiper's Panzers. The paratrooper was clearly a 'rear echelon
stallion', Peiper told himself; and although he was one rank
higher than the SS Colonel, he didn't hesitate. He turned his
full anger on the man, who indeed had just taken over the 9th
after years in the Air Ministry at Berlin. After all, the fool was
holding up his dash for Huy, and behind him was piling up the
weight of the Sixth SS Panzer Army.

The Colonel protested that the woods to his front were
filled with Americans. From heavily fortified underground
bunkers they were fighting back fiercely. Peiper's lips curled
in a sneer. Outside it was as silent as the grave.

'Have you personally reconnoitred the American positions
in the woods?' he asked.

The Colonel, whose sole decoration was the War Service
Cross, 3rd Class, while Peiper, half his age, had won virtually
every German decoration for bravery there was, said, 'No, I
got my information from one of my battalion commanders.'

Peiper snorted, and insisted on being put in touch with the
battalion commander. Minutes later the major in question

admitted that he had received his information about the supposed Ami defences from one of his company commanders, a captain. Peiper demanded to speak to the captain. The latter revealed that he, personally, had not seen the American fortifications in the woods to the rear of Lanzerath. One of his sergeants, however. . . .

Peiper slammed down the field telephone in disgust. It was all too obvious what was going on. The 9th Parachute Regiment was fighting a nine-to-five war, only too glad to get in from the dark and cold, seeing Amis where there were none, and happy to do so.

He made his decisions. He would advance straight to his front, heading through the string of Belgian villages to the west till he reached the main motor road at Werbomont. From there he would make his dash for Huy and the River Meuse. Now he *ordered* the badly scared para Colonel to give him one of his three battalions. He needed it for his attack – if there was to be any need for an attack, and somehow he suspected there wasn't.

By just after three on the morning of Sunday, 17 December, his mixed force of paras and tanks were crawling through the darkness towards the 'strongly defended, fortified American positions' in the woods beyond Lanzerath. The task force met with no resistance whatsoever, apart from scattered rifle fire. The Amis had fled, all save one: a radio operator who, hidden in a cellar, counted the Germans as they passed and notified the rear of what was coming their way: 30 German tanks, 28 half-tracks and long columns of infantry, all heading westwards. The attack was moving again, and, apart from a handful of engineers and COMZ* troops, there was nothing to stop them reaching Huy.

Two hours later at five o'clock that morning, Skorzeny was awakened from his sleep by an excited orderly. Dietrich's HQ had just reported that Peiper had captured Honsfeld and was moving towards the village of Büllingen, where there was a huge petrol and oil dump. Panzerbrigade 150 had to be

---

* US rear area command

alerted immediately to move into Belgium to follow Peiper up. The drive to the Meuse bridges was on again!

On the morning of Sunday, 17 December, the situation in the Ardennes was this. Of the two American divisions facing the main thrust of both Dietrich's and von Manteuffel's Panzer armies, the 106th US Infantry and the 28th US Infantry, the first had two regiments cut off and virtually surrounded and the second had one regiment heavily engaged and badly disorganised. To the rear of both, their commanding officers, General Jones and General Cota, had little control or know-ledge of their men at the front. In due course, most of them would surrender. This lack of control and knowledge ex-tended right up to the highest echelons and the Supreme Commander, General Eisenhower, himself.

To the north in Holland the 7th US Armoured Division had been alerted to proceed to St Vith and see what help it might be able to offer to a hard-pressed General Jones, who had had no combat experience in all his twenty-six years in the army. Now its leading units were on their way, fighting traffic jams, chaos, sabotage and panic, trying to work a path through the hundreds of men fleeing from the front in what later became known as the 'great bug-out'.

To the rear, in France, the 101st US Airborne Division, which had suffered severe casualties in the previous autumn's great paradrop into Holland, had been alerted, too. It was Eisenhower's sole reserve in the whole of the Continent. Its commanders were ordered to drive to the Ardennes and report to General Middleton, the commander of the corps so badly hit in the Ardennes, whose headquarters was at Bastogne, a town hardly anyone had ever heard of before. Soon, the name of Bastogne and what happened there would pass into American history and that defiant 'Nuts'* would become part of America's folklore, together with those other ringing phrases, 'Damn the torpedoes!' and 'I shall return!'

---

*The airborne commander's reply when asked to surrender by the German troops surrounding Bastogne. In fact, the general in question used a more down-to-earth phrase.

But on that grim Sunday, when the bottom seemed to be falling out of the nice, safe, confident Allied world, no one was thinking of the history books. On the contrary, those most immediately concerned at the front in the Ardennes were either fighting for their lives or retreating in fear and confusion – in some cases preceded by senior officers who had lost their nerve completely. In fact, the whole of General Middleton's VIIIth Corps had virtually collapsed, and although the Supreme Command did not know, already a very real danger was beginning to emerge that part of General Bradley's army group would be cut off soon if something drastic on the part of the Allies was not done.

Admittedly, the two 'shoulders' of the Bulge – in particular, the one in the north facing Dietrich's Sixth Panzer Army – were holding. But to a certain extent the Germans had anticipated that. They had no intention of breaking through all along the front. Their aim was the blitzkrieg, as of old: bold armoured thrusts deep into the heart of the enemy's defences with the flanks taking care of themselves. Their objective was the Meuse and what lay beyond, not the mere capture of useless terrain.

It was not surprising that on that day Bradley's mood changed from complacency to despondency. Arriving at his headquarters in Luxembourg on his return from Paris, he walked into the brownstone building opposite the main station, to find his G-2, General Allen, in charge of operations working on a large-scale map of the front in the Ardennes. Now, suddenly, it was covered with a rash of blue and red crayon marks, signifying enemy and American units.

Allen, his face sombre and 'brooding' (according to Bradley's later account), told him that intelligence had identified fourteen enemy divisions, half of them armoured, perhaps some 150,000 men in all.

Bradley's dismay was all too obvious. 'Pardon my French, Lev', he blurted out, 'but where in hell has the sonovabitch gotten all his strength?' Where indeed?

Two hours before Skorzeny was wakened, the armada of slow-moving Junkers transports started to cross the Belgian frontier, bearing the paras who would play their part in helping Peiper to drive for the Meuse.

At midnight the priest duly blessed their planes and crews and they took off from their two fields, with the paras in high spirits, singing the parachutists' song, '*Rot scheint die Sonne*' ('Red shines the sun'), bellowing its bold if fatalistic text:

> When Germany is in danger, there is only one thing for us to do:
> To fight, to conquer and believe we shall die.
> From our aircraft, my friend, there is no return. . . .

Gradually the singing died as the planes droned westwards, guided, on account of the inexperienced pilots, by search-lights the whole way until they had passed over the Rhine at Bonn.

Now those in the lead planes were able to see the glare of the front in the far distance to the west: the silent, flickering pink of the permanent barrage. Everywhere the pale-faced, tense officers began to rap out their order, '*Helmets on! . . . Check equipment! . . . Stand by to jump!*'

In the lead plane von der Heydte, who was jumping with one hand strapped to his side because of an accident, was making a last check to his equipment when the Junkers rocked violently. They had been spotted by Allied flak.

Suddenly the air was full of the brilliant white, hurrying spurts of tracer, curving inwards at the massed transports. Behind von der Heydte's Junkers, another plane seemed to stop in mid-air, as if held up by an invisible hand. Next instant it plummeted to the ground in a vivid orange dive.

The Baron gave a look around his plane. His men were visibly shaken. Only two out of the ten had jumped in combat before. The others were not used to the frightening confusion of an airborne landing under fire. Von der Heydte hid his own feelings and scoured the ground below for the landing beacon – a brilliant burning cross, composed of three white lights and a red one pointing westwards. Fifteen minutes later he spotted it. They were exactly on time and target (unknown to the Baron, his plane was probably the only one to be in this fortunate position).

Now the green light at the door started to wink alarmingly.

The paras shuffled forward, feeling the icy cold air from the open door buffet their scared faces. Von der Heydte positioned himself in the opening. Below, the ground raced by, hurrying dizzy patches of black interspersed by the white of the snow.

Abruptly a hard hand hit his shoulder. '*Los!*' the dispatcher cried. He went out in a rush. The wind gripped him and seemed about to drag him down to his death. He was falling at a tremendous rate. Suddenly there was a dry crack. He gave a great gasp as the parachute jerked at his chest. Almost miraculously his mad progress was halted. Above him the strange Russian chute billowed out and he was drifting towards the ground, already in the grip of a new danger, the wind. According to the experts the wind velocity at ground level should have been 20 feet per second. In fact it was more than 50, and now von der Heydte fought with all his strength not to drift too far from the DZ.

A thick fir forest, typical of the area, swung into sight. At the very last moment it slid away. Now his triangular parachute was oscillating at a tremendous rate. He lost control. The ground came racing up to meet him. Next moment he hit it, hard, and blacked out briefly.

A few moments later he came to again – to find himself completely alone!

There was no sound now, save that of the wind in the firs. The drone of the Junkers' engines had died away, as they turned and headed east once more. To von der Heydte, it was as if he were the last man on earth. It was Crete in May, 1941 all over again, when he had found himself, his battalion vanished, one man, it had seemed, against the whole of the British army. Then he had found his men quickly; now von der Heydte was destined to be alone for a long time.

What had happened? It had been a combination of several factors, the inexperience of the 'Stalingrad Squadron's' pilots, the American flak and the high wind. Out of the total of 106 pilots, only thirty-five dropped their men in the right place. The rest started dropping the paras after they passed Bonn, nearly 100 miles away from the real DZ. The wind and the inexperience of the majority of the paras did the rest.

They came down all over the place, carried far off course by the high wind, landing in little groups or alone in those snowy wastes, many of them with broken legs and arms, their weapons and equipment lost, totally out of touch with their unit, their mission forgotten now in their misery, longing only for the sound of a human voice, even if it were American.

Sergeant Lingelbach was a veteran paratrooper. He had made hundreds of jumps, though his only combat jump had been at Stavanger, Norway, in April, 1940, when after two hours the paras had been welcomed by their own fire-and-drum corps. Since then Lingelbach had fought as an infantry-man in Russia. Now on the morning of 17 December he found himself alone, hanging from a fir tree 6 feet above the ground, and every time he tried to move his left arm, a stab of pain ran through his whole body. It was definitely broken.

Somehow, in spite of his broken arm, Sergeant Lingelbach freed himself from the tree, and prepared to move westwards where he had seen a large number of chutes come floating down. Now he began moving in that direction along the bank of a frozen stream, one of the many which ran through the marshy *Hohes Venn** of that part of Belgium. But he had not gone far when he came across another parachute, and in the grey light of the new dawn he could make out another figure in the coveralls of the paratroops. He had found a comrade, but Lingelbach's joy was soon quenched when the man on the ground told him, 'Both my legs are broken.'

Lingelbach told the other man of his own injury and the latter said quite bluntly, 'Then you must find the rest and get on with the job. . . . Only first do me the favour of putting a bullet through my head!'

Lingelbach refused. He decided to stay with his wounded comrade, but keep an eye open for the rest. All that long miserable day he stayed with the gravely wounded man, somehow keeping him alive. In the end he decided he had had enough. He would tow his wounded friend on a makeshift sledge to the nearest American position and surrender.

---

* Roughly, 'High Country'

Under the existing circumstances, there would be no dis-
honour in doing so, he told himself.

One day later Lingelbach and the other para, named
Wiertz, completely exhausted but alive, were found sprawled
out in the snow by a German reconnaissance unit. A little
later, while Lingelbach was recovering in a front-line hospital, it was captured by the Americans. Thus it came that the
sergeant, one of the few survivors, was able to tell his tale to a
sympathetic American doctor.

Many of the young paras were never found. The bog
dragged them down for ever. Others were found only years
later, as skeletons, discovered by search teams sent out by the
Belgian authorities. A few were fortunate enough to become
prisoners of war almost immediately.

Just before dawn von der Heydte had collected some six men,
four teen-age privates, a young lieutenant and one sergeant
with a twisted ankle. Together this sorry little group out of a
force of 1,200 paras made its way through the freezing
darkness to the crossroads leading to Malmedy, Eupen and
Verviers. As dawn broke another twenty-odd made their way
to join up with the Baron and his tiny force hiding in the
ditches on both sides of the crossroads, freezing and shaking
in the icy grey light. Almost as soon as they had exchanged
experiences, there was the sound of heavy motors grinding up
the long, winding hill road that led from Eupen, the Headquarters of the US Vth Corps. Before the paras, numbed by
cold and slow-witted, could go to ground, the first of the
trucks, packed with American infantrymen, came round the
bend.

But the Amis did not fire. Instead, they waved at the men in
the rimless helmets and camouflaged capes and uniforms
shivering there in the ditches. Obviously they took them for
their own troops, and were comforted by the thought that
their own people were in position up here in these remote
heights as they drove southwards to meet the threat posed by
the Sixth SS Panzer Army's thrust to the west. Startled, the
paras waved back.

That was the first of many convoys containing men of the
7th US Armoured Division and some of the 1st US Infantry

Division, 'the Big Red One', being rushed to stop Peiper's bold drive for the Meuse and the bridge at Huy.

Miserably, von der Heydte watched the long convoys roll on and on, unable to stop them with the 125 men now at his disposal. With his full command of 1,200 paras at his command he could have made an effective job of sealing off the vital crossroads. He might well have been able to hold it for two days, as Kraemer had demanded. But not now. He was too weak, and his men had nothing but their rifles and machine pistols, with what ammunition they could carry. It would be a pointless massacre to attempt to hold the crossroads with that kind of force. In the end von der Heydte decided to withdraw further into the marshy fenland and think things over. Already, though, the Bavarian aristocrat knew in his heart of hearts that Operation 'Auk' was a miserable failure. All the effort, all the self-sacrifice, had been for nothing. The last German parachute operation of World War II was a mess. His arm broken, his feet frozen, his stomach already rumbling with hunger, Baron von der Heydte concluded that there were only two alternatives left to him now: retreat back to his own lines – or surrender.

Little did the perplexed Baron know that the abortive jump would help to trigger off a Europe-wide panic of major proportions, with civilians and soldiers seeing German paratroopers everywhere; with rumour after rumour, one more exaggerated than the next, spreading like wild-fire and causing more panic and disruption than the landing of a whole airborne division behind American lines. It was going to be May 1940 all over again.

Unknown to von der Heydte, his paras had landed over a huge area, being carried hither and thither by that 15-m.p.h. ground wind. In the north they landed behind the British lines in Holland beyond Maastricht, and in the south sightings of German paratroops were reported as far afield as Verdun and Epinal. Even the 300 straw dummies contributed to the panic, for, with no paratrooper to direct the shroud lines, they were carried far into the Allied hinterland.

Now reports of para-landings were flooding into Allied front-line headquarters everywhere. Wild rumours circulated almost immediately, and continued to circulate even after the war. In his book, *The Last Phase* (1946), author Walter Millis has General 'Blood an' Guts' Patton fighting his way north to the Ardennes through 'massed German parachutists'. In Eisenhower's *Story of the War* (late 1945) he reports that 'parties of paratroops were dropped throughout the battle area', which was untrue, as we have seen.

Almost immediately, jittery American staff officers began to react (and not only the Americans, but Belgians and French too). Up in Eupen, 5 miles from where von der Heydte was now hiding with his pathetic band, the whole of a combat command, some 3,000 armoured infantrymen of the 3rd US Armoured Division were put on immediate parachute alert. Further back, at Liège, the US reinforcement depots turfed out all their infantry, cooks, clerks – anybody who could hold a rifle – and sent them to the outskirts of the big Belgian industrial town on the Meuse to defend it to the last against German paratroops.

Further back, at General Hodges' HQ at the casino town of Spa, reports were flooding in of para-landings everywhere in the rear area. Outside Hodges' HQ at the Hôtel Britannique, the vehicles, laden with personal possessions, were already beginning to line up, as staff officers panicked and prepared to join 'the great bug-out'. It wouldn't be long before First US Army HQ joined the flight westwards.

It was the same beyond the Meuse and deep into Belgium and northern France. Hastily, the Allied flags and the portraits of Churchill, de Gaulle and Roosevelt, which the day before had seemed to decorate every window, were snatched down. Parents forbad their children, especially the girls, to talk to Allied soldiers. The black market between the Allies and the civilians came to an abrupt stop. Everyone knew that the Germans had their para-agents everywhere and did not want to feature on some 'automatic arrest' list, once the dreaded gentlemen in their ankle-length leather coats and dark, broad-brimmed felt hats made their appearance yet again. For one did not need a crystal ball to know that the Gestapo was coming back!

Now, in the phrase of Jean Cocteau, when Western Europe had been gripped by a similar fifth-column mania, the general

public 'spied nuns doing up their garters behind every bush'.*
Based on memories of that terrible May of 1940, the
obsession was understandable. The myth of the ubiquitous
German drew no distinction between military drops and the
infiltration of a few agents by parachute. People remembered
the successful German para-glider landing on the forts of
Eben-Emael outside Liège and the virtual capture of Holland
by widespread paradrops under the command of General
Student.

General Strong reported accurately on 17 December
towards evening: 'Enemy parachutists have dropped behind
the lines in an area not yet clearly defined but including
Verviers. Their strength is estimated to be about 1,500.'
Further, Patton's Third Army G-2 stated categorically on that
same day 'that the objective of the paras' attack was to control
the cross-roads on the Eupen-Malmédy road'. Indeed, the files
of front-line units for that and subsequent days are filled with
hundreds of reports of sightings of German paratroops. In
spite of them all, however, no one was listening.

Despite the total failure, militarily speaking, of Baron von
der Heydte's parachute drop, its psychological effect was
tremendous. All along the Ghost front and deep into the
hinterland, it added even more to the existing confusion
caused by the surprise counter-attack, and addled yet further
the nerves of already jittery staffs. Commanders and men
began to see paratroopers stalking through the wintry fields
towards them on all sides. A great panic was in the making –
and there was worse to come!

---

* Then it was widely thought that the Germans had parachuted their men
in disguised as nuns, and it was ordered that any suspicious-looking nun
should be stripped, to the waist only, to ascertain whether or not she had
the tell-tale red marks of a parachute harness around 'her' shoulders.

TWO

The Big Flap

<hr>

1

By the morning of Monday, 18 December, there were more than fifty German armoured columns probing into the Ardennes. Some, in the north, had gone a mere mile. To the south of the Bulge, however, most had penetrated 10 to 12 miles, while one of von Manteuffel's Fifth Army divisions had raced 30 miles, deep into the heart of the American rear.

Of Dietrich's SS formations, the armoured column commanded by Obersturmbannführer Jochen Peiper of the 1st SS, the '*Leibstandarte*'*, had been the most successful. He had bullied, pleaded, cajoled and battled his 5,000-strong force deep behind US lines and was now preparing to assault the river town of Stavelot. By nightfall Peiper had successfully accomplished that mission, and was pushing on out of the Ardennes, heading for the Meuse, coming ever closer to the headquarters of no less a person than the commander of the First US Army, General Courtney Hodges.

Now Spa, the little Belgian town which housed the Army HQ, was in complete uproar. Everywhere the side roads leading on to the broad boulevard westwards were clogged with jeeps, trucks, staff cars, half-tracks – anything on wheels – as the panic-stricken staff officers 'bugged out'. Inside the town hall, the mayor ordered that all Allied flags should be

<hr>

*The 'bodyguard'

removed before the Germans arrived and nineteen Belgians imprisoned on collaboration charges should be released immediately; the frightened Belgian did not want to end up in those same cells himself once the Gestapo was back.

Richard Hottelet of CBS (Columbia Broadcasting System) radio recorded observing one 'weary staff officer, putting down one receiver and lifting another' and mumbling to him, 'It sounds like the Stock Market crash in 1929.' Another, James Cassidy of NBC (National Broadcasting Company) radio recorded:

> I will never forget the experience of conquest in reverse. The wild cheers of welcome accorded the American liberators three months ago had turned to ashes. Most civilians stood around in silent groups in the streets watching the mud-splattered army trucks moving. American flags were being removed from some of the shop windows and so were forbidden Belgian banners. As I left I wondered how long it would be until Nazi banners once again adorned those windows which for three months had displayed the Stars and Stripes.

As Captain Merriam of Ninth Army, attached to the 7th Armoured Division, summed it up, as he joined 'the great bug-out' for the new First Army HQ at Chaudfontaine near Liège (from which it would flee once more, ever westwards, within three days); 'It's no fun to be on the losing team, especially when a pale, wan, dazed civilian says, "And what is to become of us?"'

Now General Hodges was virtually alone in the big, echoing Hôtel Britannique, its windows flung open through which his officers had tossed their kit to the waiting vehicles below, the lights blazing in spite of blackout regulations. We do not know his thoughts. We do know, however, that the tall, courteous former infantryman realised he had suffered a major defeat in the Ardennes.

Ten thousand men of his 106th Division had been trapped in the hills and would surrender within the next twenty-four hours, the second biggest surrender of American troops since the Civil War. St Vith was surrounded, and the 7th US Armoured Division sent there to help the 106th was fighting for its life instead. Further to the south, von Manteuffel's armoured columns, having broken through virtually everywhere, were now racing for the second most important rail-and-road head (St Vith was the other) east of the River Meuse, Bastogne. By midnight they had cut all approach roads to the town, and the week-long siege of what later became known as 'Nuts City' commenced in all its horror.*

All that Hodges had to offer in the way of additional manpower to stop this massive German armoured drive was the lightly armed 101st Airborne, most of it still battling its way across a snow-bound France towards Bastogne. That day it must have seemed to Hodges that his world had fallen apart.

At 3 p.m. General Hodges was informed that Peiper's column was already beginning to drive out from Stavelot and was heading for Spa. Barring its way there was only one road-block and a few half-tracks. Hodges made his decision. He ordered whoever was left at the Britannique to the east of Spa to help the handful of defenders. He, himself would leave now for Chaudfontaine. Gathering up a few papers, he let his Chief-of-Intelligence Colonel 'Monk' Dickson lead him through the big salon on the second floor where Kaiser Wilhelm had signed his abdication in 1918 when Hodges had been a captain of infantry fighting in France. Now, as a full general in command of over a quarter of a million men, he too, in his way, was abdicating.

On that grey, grim Monday, there was only one bright spot on the whole American front: that flamboyant 'cowboy general', as Hitler called him, pistol-packing 'Blood an' Guts' Patton, the commander of the US Third Army, which was located in northern France. About the time Hodges decided to leave Spa, he was closeted with General Bradley at his HQ in Luxembourg. Already Patton had realised that something was seriously wrong up in the First Army. Now he faced a very worried Bradley, who showed him the situation map, covered with a rash of newly identified German units in the Ardennes, some of them not more than 10 miles away from where they

---

* Its local name, based on that famous reply to the German demand for surrender.

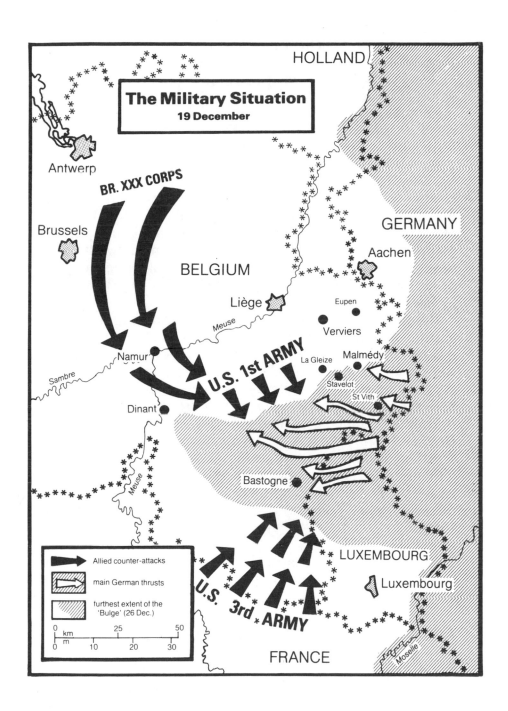

The Military Situation
19 December

HOLLAND

Antwerp

BR. XXX CORPS

Brussels

BELGIUM

GERMANY

Aachen

Liège

Eupen

Verviers

Meuse

U.S. 1st ARMY

La Gleize

Malmédy

Namur

Stavelot

Sambre

St Vith

Dinant

Bastogne

LUXEMBOURG

Luxembourg

➤ Allied counter-attacks

main German thrusts

furthest extent of the
'Bulge' (26 Dec.)

U.S.

3rd ARMY

0   25   50
 km
0   10   20   30
 m

FRANCE

Moselle

121

were then located. The whole American line appeared to be sagging like a dam about to burst.

'I feel you won't like what we are going to do,' Bradley said warily, for once Patton had been his superior before he had been relieved of his command for having struck a shell-shocked soldier in Sicily, and Bradley lived in awe of his former boss. 'But I fear it is necessary.'

Patton knew what was coming. He would have to break off his own Third Army attack to aid Hodges' First. Without hesitation, he volunteered his favourite armoured division, the 4th Armoured Division, plus the 80th Infantry Division. He would start them moving north to Luxembourg at mid-night. 'I can also alert the 26th to start moving in twenty-four hours, if necessary,' he said in that strange, high-pitched voice of his which contrasted so markedly with his rugged 6 foot 2 inches of masculinity.

Bradley was obviously pleased with Patton's spontaneous gesture, and the latter set off back to his HQ at Nancy, driving through the dark, which Patton hated, especially as the roads were now patrolled by highly nervous and trigger-happy MPs. Arriving there, he was told by his chief-of-staff that Bradley had been on the phone. He was to start rolling his divisions northwards immediately and not to waste a moment's time. Brad also wanted to talk to him again.

At eight that night, Patton managed to get through, although the lines had been cut everywhere, to be told by Bradley, 'The situation up there is much worse than when I talked to you. You and a staff officer are to meet me at Verdun for a conference with General Eisenhower tomorrow morning at eleven.'

Now Patton knew that if Eisenhower was coming up the situation was really serious – in his words, 'The shit has really hit the fan!'

Tension and nervousness were now in the very air. The news flooding back from the front was bad. The Germans had broken through at half-a-dozen points up there; and there seemed no stopping them. Everywhere the roads were clogged with men fleeing westwards.

It was no different to the rear. Now every crossroads and

bridge were manned by teams flung together hastily consisting of American soldiers, French and Belgian conscripts, clad in the cast-offs of four Allied armies, as well as the local gendarmerie in their high, blue, old-fashioned shakos – that is, those who had not fled westwards themselves.

Manning one such road-block outside Liège after being hurriedly turfed out of the local 'repple-depple'* Staff Sergeant Giles was very angry at his sudden change of circumstances. His diary reveals his anger, which was typical of the emotions of many American soldiers that freezing December day:

> Cold, my Lord! Snow & ice & slush underfoot & a drizzle of sleet falling. The sleet fell down your neck even with your collar up & you just hunched up & tried to keep the wind & the wet out the best way you could. Gloves too short & checking the guns every now & then soon got wet then froze. Feet were soaked inside of half an hour. I don't have any overshoes & my shoes leak like a sieve.

But it was not just the tedium and weather which worried Staff Sergeant Giles of the US Engineers and many like him that day; it was the tension and uncertainty, as they waited for the Germans to come down the road they were supposed to be protecting. He went on: '. . . all tensed up, looking & listening, thinking every vehicle we heard – and what a hell of a lot of them there were – was a Kraut. Everything that moved scared the living hell out of us. Don't know whether I shook worse from cold or fear!'

Not far from Staff Sergeant Giles, another such freezing road block, near the Meuse at the hamlet of Aywaille, was defended by a mixed bunch of black US Service troops and white MPs. According to one British report by Brigadier Essame of the 43rd Infantry Division, one had to be particularly wary of these 'coloured troops', who had 'already shot one American and two Belgians'.

In the segregated US army of those days, when both Patton and Eisenhower talked of their black troops as 'darkies and niggahs', such trigger-happy behaviour was expected of

---

* US army slang for a reinforcement depot

blacks; it was thought that they were easily scared and quick to panic. This attitude towards them was of course shared by the German enemy, the *Herrenvolk*, with their myth of racial superiority.

Now, however, on this cold December day, those 'darkies' were going to play a role of great significance in the Big Flap which had already started. If he had known their true worth, Adolf Hitler would surely have awarded all of them the Iron Cross, First Class, for their unwitting assistance to the German cause.

About noon a jeep slowly started to approach the road-block. It contained three men in American uniform. Dutifully it began to slow down as the men at the barrier raised their weapons and one of the 'snowdrops' stepped out into the middle of the road, hand upraised, carbine still slung across his back.

The jeep driver braked, there was a small exchange in English and then the MP asked for the password.

The driver paled and stuttered something.

'*The password*, buddy!' the MP rasped threateningly, as the black soldiers of the COMZ stared at the jeep's three occupants with sudden interest.

The jeep driver blustered something about not having been given a password.

That was enough for the MP. Each man in the Liège area who was travelling that day *had* been given a password before leaving his outfit. He indicated that the three Pfc's in the jeep should get out – slowly.

Swiftly the identities of these three Americans who didn't know the password were established. They were Pfc Charles W. Lawrence, Pfc George Sensenbach and Pfc Clarence van der Werth. Nothing very special about that.

Now the black soldiers began to examine the jeep, and almost immediately it was discovered that these were no ordinary GIs; for in the rear, hidden under the seat, they found a huge roll of one-hundred dollar bills, as fresh as the day they had come off the printing presses – which wasn't surprising; they had been printed the week before in the secret German concentration camp forgery plant!

For a little while the searchers suspected that they had

apprehended a group of deserters or black marketeers; the three did speak excellent English. But not for long. Soon they dug up in the interior of the jeep two British sten machine pistols, two Colts, two German Walther pistols, plastic explosive, a radio transmitter, six American hand grenades, and most incriminating of all, the cigarette lighters containing poison, the L (for 'lethal') pill.

Now the smallest of the three started talking. His real name wasn't George Sensenbach, but Wilhelm Schmidt, and he was a corporal in the German army! It was the sensation of the day. The black and white soldiers crowded around him, as he explained how he and the other two had set off from Monschau in Germany on the twelfth.

Some days later, they related, they had successfully penetrated the US lines, posing as members of the 5th US Armoured Division, with their mission of 'infiltrating through the Americans and reporting the condition of the Meuse bridges and of the roads leading to those bridges'.

The soldiers didn't wait to hear any more. They raced for the field phones. They got in contact with Liège HQ. There were gasps of excitement at the other end. More Kraut infiltrators! They had to be everywhere! Within thirty minutes, a fleet of jeeps crammed with heavily armed MPs and members of American field intelligence, the CIC, were on their way to interrogate the three ashen-faced Germans who had less than a week to live before they were tied to stakes in the little Belgian township of Henri-Chapelle, a matter of miles away from the homeland they would never see again, and shot to death as spies.

Now forty years later it is not known what methods the CIC used on the three Germans to make them talk. American intelligence was not particularly squeamish at the best of times. They were, after all, living in the days of the 'third degree', standard police practice back home in the States, and higher headquarters were screaming out for reliable information about these German infiltrators who seemed to be everywhere this third week of December, with the front crumbling away disastrously. So they made the Germans talk – and what a tale they had to tell!

Schmidt, who had been one of the first volunteers to join Skorzeny, told his impatient interrogators, 'Early in November 1944, I reported to an SS camp at Friedenthal, where I was examined as to my linguistic ability by a board consisting of an SS, a Luftwaffe, and a naval officer. I passed the test, but was ordered to refresh my English. For this purpose I spent three weeks at prisoner-of-war camps in Küstrin and Limburg, where large numbers of American troops were being held.' Later, Schmidt explained, he was posted to Gräfenwohr, where he was placed in a special unit. Here 'Our training consisted of studying the organisation of the American army, identification of American insignia, American drill and linguistic exercises.' Now Schmidt really had the CIC men sitting on the edges of their seats, for he told how the engineers in his group had the task of 'destroying headquarters and headquarters personnel'.

'What headquarters and what headquarters personnel?' the CIC wanted to know.

Now it all came out, those wild rumours that had run the rounds of Gräfenwohr the month before: the dash across France disguised as German POWs to break into Lorient; the surprise attack on Montgomery's headquarters in Holland; the column of 'captured' Tiger tanks to meet up with the assassins assembling at the Café de la Paix. . . .

'To do what?' the CIC agents undoubtedly asked excitedly.

'To kill . . . General . . . *Eisenhower!*'

One can almost imagine the unfortunate German's listeners exploding at that, as they put it all together. Skorzeny, wasn't he the guy who rescued Mussolini in 1943 and attempted to bump off Tito a year later? Didn't he also, only months ago, kidnap young Horthy, the son of the Hungarian dictator?

Of course, these Krauts disguised as Americans were hired killers – why else all the weapons and the suicide pills? – out to meet up with their scar-faced SS boss in Paris. From there the whole murderous bunch of them would swarm out, like the rats they were, to Eisenhower's headquarters at Versailles to kill the Supreme Commander.

Ike had to be warned at once!

2

The von der Heydte para-drop, and now the first of Skorzeny's commandos apprehended and 'telling all', did it. The Great Flap commenced almost immediately – and right at the top, in Supreme Allied Headquarters at Paris!

Colonel Gordon Sheen, Eisenhower's Counter-intelligence Chief, decided at once that Corporal Schmidt's story could not be ignored. He commanded that Eisenhower should be given complete protection (up to now he had travelled around freely with only an orderly and a driver for protection) and moved immediately from his private quarters at the Petit Trianon, which had been von Rundstedt's up to the summer and which the Germans knew intimately, to a safer place. Thereupon Colonel Baldwin B. Smith, who was regarded as a perfect double of Eisenhower, was abruptly promoted to five-star general and doubled for Eisenhower right up until Christmas.

From the 20 to 26 December, while a desperate battle raged at the front, involving nearly three million men, Eisenhower was a prisoner in his own headquarters, cut off from the decision-making process. As his secretary–mistress, shrewd, hard-faced, green-eyed Kay Summersby recorded:

> Security officers immediately turned headquarters compound into a virtual fortress. Barbed wire appeared. Several tanks moved in. The normal guard was doubled, trebled, quadrupled. The pass system became a matter of life and death instead of the old formality. The sound of a car exhaust was enough to halt work in every office, to start a flurry of telephone calls to our office, to inquire whether the boss was all right. The atmosphere was worse than that of a combat headquarters up at the front, where everyone knows how to take such a situation in their stride.

General Strong protested personally that Sheen was going too far. He was overruled. Eisenhower would have 'to obey orders'. Now Ike was guarded by a whole battalion of MPs. Once he simply walked out of his office, mumbling angrily to Kay Summersby, 'Hell's fire, I'm going for a walk. If anyone

wants to shoot me, he can go right ahead. I've got to get out!'
And walk he did, followed by a whole company of heavily
armed, helmeted, suspicious-eyed MPs.

Sleep seemed impossible. As Kay Summersby wrote in her
diary: 'I lay awake for hours envisioning death and worse at
the hands of SS agents. Sleep was impossible. With the tramp,
tramp, tramp of heavy-booted guards patrolling our tin roof.'

Captain Harry S. Butcher, a former vice-president of CBS
and now a kind of public relations man for Eisenhower, was
allowed to visit the imprisoned Eisenhower, and told the
General of how he had been stopped by road blocks everywhere on his way back from the front. He found Eisenhower
thoroughly irritated by the restrictions on his moves: 'There
are all sorts of guards, some with machine-guns, around the
house, and he has to go to and fro from the office, led, and
sometimes, followed by an armed guard in a jeep. He seemed
pleased to have someone to talk with like me, from the
outside world.'

Butcher, a genial man on informal terms with Eisenhower,
joked with his boss just before he left, 'Now you know how it
must feel to be President and always under the watchful eye of
the Secret Service.'

One wonders if, eight years later when he was elected
President of the United States, Eisenhower remembered that
quip and where it was made?

Now the scare spread from Supreme Allied Headquarters to
Paris itself. A rigorous curfew was enforced and the capital
put out of bounds to all US servicemen on leave. Suddenly the
Place Pigalle ('Pig Alley' to GIs on leave) was deserted of its
lounging doughboys and the French tarts in their little
rabbit-fur jackets and cork-heeled wedge shoes. Now the only
Americans seen in the streets were grim-faced security men
on duty, searching for the would-be killers hired by Skorzeny,
the man who had now been labelled 'Public Enemy Number
One'.

French police. Naturally at that 'damned Café de la Paix', as
Skorzeny was to curse it in years to come, the CIC set up a
permanent ambush, complete with guns and tanks, lying in
wait for the killers to rendezvous there, presumably with

'Public Enemy Number One' at their head. Security in Paris was so tight that even generals were stopped and sometimes arrested. General Hughes, Eisenhower's 'eyes and ears', who did a lot of private snooping for the Supreme Commander, was twice refused permission to enter his own Paris hotel because the sentries didn't recognise him. That evening, he stomped in rage to see the *Folies Bergères* with his current girl friend – and damned to the eight o'clock curfew for all American troops!

Another American general, jug-eared, bear-like General Littlejohn, returned to his quarters at the Hotel Astoria and found it swarming with sentries armed with fixed bayonets, who frequently hampered the irate General's movement. In despair, he cried to one of his worried officers, 'Let's do away with them [the sentries]. If any Germans come, just send them up to me. *I'll* take care of them!' But Littlejohn was one of the very few who didn't take the Skorzeny scare seriously. The whole of Europe was awash with rumours and half-truths, with people turning to the German radio stations for the first time in years to find out 'the truth'. For in his first guilty panic at being caught by surprise by the German counter-attack, Eisenhower had ordered a total news black-out for forty-eight hours.

Spies, saboteurs, killers and para-agents were spotted everywhere, and hundreds of innocent American soldiers were arrested because guards or sentries didn't like the look of them or they didn't give the 'right' answer when challenged.

Big, bluff Brigadier Bruce Clarke, in the midst of a last-ditch defence of the town of St Vith with what was left of the 7th Armoured Division, was 'arrested', for example, on the morning of 20 December by American military policemen.

Over and over he repeated, 'But I'm General Bruce Clarke of the CCB [Combat Command B].'

'Like hell!' the MPs snarled cynically. 'You're one of Skorzeny's men. We were told to watch out for a Kraut posing as a one-star general.'

While Clarke raged, knowing that the vital rail and road head of St Vith might well be lost while he was in gaol, the MPs kept him in custody for five long hours. In the end the

MPs did release him and one of them had the audacity to ask for his autograph.

Nonplussed, Clarke gave him it, too.

Clarke was not the only senior officer to be stopped. His commander, General Bradley, recalled later, 'Three times I was ordered to prove my identity by cautious GIs. The first time by identifying Springfield as the capital of Illinois (my questioner held out for Chicago); the second time by locating the guard between the centre and tackle on a line of scrimmage; the third time by naming the then current spouse of a blonde named Betty Grable. Grable stopped me, but the sentry did not. Pleased at having stumped me, he nevertheless passed me on.'

Montgomery was another victim, and in despair, finally, he pleaded with General Simpson of the US Ninth Army to provide him with American identity documents so that he could go about his business of trying to re-establish the front in the north.

As General Bradley was to comment, 'A half million GIs played cat and mouse with each other each time they met on the road. Neither rank nor credentials spared the traveller an inquisition at each intersection he passed.'

Now on all sides, American tried to trick American. Soldiers on the road would find themselves stopped and a tommy-gun thrust menacingly through the frosted window of their jeep or truck, with a hoarse voice demanding, 'Okay, buddy, who's dem bums? . . . . 'Who is Pruneface? . . . . Where does Li'l Abner live? . . . Who works with Jiggs?'

Others, knowing the German's difficulty with 'r's' and 'w's', tried out intricate tongue-twisters on the suspect, using those letters, 'Rotund Rosie runs round rugged rocks. . . . William wilted visibly when Vera whipped off her woollies', and the like.

Skorzeny's and von der Heydte's operations were paying off a thousand-fold in a manner that the two colonels had never imagined. The British-run 'German' radio station, *Soldatensender Calais*, reported that more than 250 of Skorzeny's men had been captured, although only the three of Corporal Schmidt's unfortunate team had actually been apprehended. We shall never know who the other 247 unfortunates were. Radio Nice stated that a local bank had been looted by Skorzeny paras – some 400 miles away from the scene of the fighting! The Conservative *Daily Telegraph* informed its true-blue Tory readers, in all seriousness, that specially trained women agents under Skorzeny's control had been dropped in the Paris area where they were to seduce US soldiers. Once the latter had been duly 'seduced' and presumably had 'revealed all', they were to be killed by the handy little dagger which every German Mata Hari carried in her purse!

Trying to plug the gap in the line made by Peiper's SS, now bottled up in the hill-village of La Gleize, General James Gavin of the US 101st Airborne was discussing his mission at Hodges' HQ when a staff offlcer walked in and handed a field message to the Chief-of-Staff. The message turned out to be an important piece of information from an NCO who had been guarding a bridge across the River Salm at Stavelot. A reconnaissance unit, according to the unknown NCO, had arrived from the 1st SS and destroyed his bridge.

The message made Hodges – and, naturally, Gavin – believe that the SS reconnaissance unit was ordered to cover the westward advance of a major formation, for which purpose it had to destroy the bridge.

Then Gavin, a youthful paratroop veteran, thought the message 'reassuring'. Later he found out to his cost that it was neither reassuring nor accurate, and it remained for him 'one of the many minor mysteries of the early stages of the Battle of the Bulge'. In fact, the bridge at Stavelot had not been blown up, and at that moment was the centre of the German force intent on linking up with Peiper.

Had the unknown sergeant been yet another victim of the great spy scare? No one ever found out.

It was no different in the 2nd US Armoured Division, the famed 'Hell on Wheels'. Ordered about that time to move into action to help its hard-pressed comrades in the Ardennes, a leading unit turned back because, as it reported later, it 'had been ordered to do so by an American officer'.

But no 'American officer' was ever discovered throughout the Division who claimed to have given that order. Again a figment of an excited imagination, a sign of mass hysteria? Who knows?

Far to the south, Patton's Third Army reported similar strange sightings. As Patton recorded in his diary, 'On this day, four Germans in one of our jeeps, dressed in American uniforms, were killed, and another group of seventeen, also in American uniforms, were reported by 35 Division as follows: one sentinel, reinforced, saw seventeen Germans in American uniforms. Fifteen were killed – and two died suddenly.' It was a typical Patton entry, that 'two died suddenly'. But no one ever successfully identified those 'Germans', if they were indeed such.

The panic was not confined to the American forces either. The British flapped a little too, although they made fun of the great scare at the Americans' expense. A number of innocent American officers who went to visit their girl friends north of Maastricht for Christmas were arrested by the British and spent the festive season behind bars. Even one of Montgomery's 'eyes and ears', the young British and American officers whom the 'Master' used to supply him with information direct from the front – an American, in this instance – was arrested because he didn't seem to have the right answers.

It was no different in the Canadian sector of the line. British Corporal Alexander McKee, then serving with a Canadian headquarters at the Dutch town of Tilburg, made a number of entries in his diary for that grim week of the Black Christmas recording the general sense of jumpiness and downright panic in some cases. On Christmas Eve, for example, he noted that it was reported that 'two German officers were caught in the town square, dressed as Canadians – but with their gaiters fastened the wrong way round!' Two days later, he records a whole battalion of German airborne troops being dropped just outside Tilburg and Breda – which wasn't true, of course. 'None penetrated to the centre of Tilburg,' he wrote. 'However 5 German paratroops were picked up in the centre – 3 dressed as clergy, 2 in British uniform.'

A young Dutch journalist picked up in the great scare by the Canadians told him confidentially after his release that 'in the guardroom were eight German parachutists – two in regulation parachutists' uniform, the rest in British uniforms or civilian clothes. The two in German uniform were wreathed in smiles and telling the others of the sticky end awaiting them while *they* were safely out of the war.'

Finally he noted at the end of this week of scares and sudden alarms, 'Next day a parachutist was reported picked up in the local dancehall known as "Hell's Kitchen" because if you wanted a dance you had to mark your girl well in advance and shove her out on the floor as the band-leader raised his baton; that way, you got in two steps before the mob became solid. Now, "Hell's Kitchen" was even funnier because we all had to go armed and therefore handed in at the cloakroom one's rifle, pistol or sub-machine gun before entering the hall.'

Shades of the old West!

Still incidents kept happening which added fresh fuel to the Big Flap, and which proved that there *were* genuine saboteurs and agents at liberty far behind Allied lines. By now Montgomery was moving his XXXth Corps under General Horrocks down to the western bank of the River Meuse to form a barrier of British troops if the Germans managed to break through those last few miles which separated them from the key waterway. At Dinant, a scratch force of British tankers, US engineers, and Negro service corps men had been formed into a last-ditch force to defend the bridge across the Meuse there that week.

On the first evening of the establishment of this force, with the air icy cold and snow forecast, this force under Colonel Brown awaited the arrival of the first of the Panzers and the commencement of the desperate struggle for the bridge. Reasoning that the Germans would approach the town from the south, Colonel Brown had thrown a thin cordon of troops over the road where the approach road had to pass through an opening cut through solid rock. There his attached American engineers had strung a necklace of Hawkins anti-tank grenades across the road and erected a strong-point some yards to the front of the primitive minefield. If any enemy armour penetrated the road-block, which was highly likely, it

was reasoned that they'd run straight on to the mines in their
triumph.

Thus the nervous little garrison of exhausted British troops
– they had rushed from Holland to meet the German threat –
and the second-line Americans waited for the assault which
was sure to come, for already they could hear the rumble of
German guns close by.

The assault did come, but in a completely different way
from what they had expected. The grey day gave way to a grey
evening. The hours passed leadenly. It was night. There was
no sound now save the rumble of heavy artillery. Suddenly
the noise of a lone vehicle alerted the waiting soldiers. At
their strong-point the engineers tensed. In spite of the biting
cold they began to sweat. Was this the enemy?

Abruptly, before anyone could react, a US jeep containing
four men barrelled in out of the darkness.

'Halt!' someone yelled. The jeep would run straight into
the daisy-chain of mines.

Too late! The jeep roared on through them. Dinant was a
matter of minutes away. Suddenly there was the dull crump of
high explosive. Scarlet flame stabbed the night. The engineers
saw the jeep rise brokenly on a wave of flame. Next moment it
came down again with a crash. It lurched to one side, tyres
burst, oil spurting from its shattered engine, flames licking its
sides.

The horrified spell was broken. The engineers doubled
forward. Hurriedly they peeled the smouldering uniforms
from the dead GIs, telling themselves that they had just
unwittingly killed four of their own guys.

But as the first man's combat jacket was pulled off, it
revealed the jagged silver run of the SS! Another of
Hauptmann Stielau's long-range jeep teams had been discovered, and again the shock of that discovery ran through
the Allied camp, bringing ever greater panic to an already
terrified Continent.

And not only to the Continent; to the United Kingdom, too.
For, although details are hard to come by, it is clear that, in
the same way that the British army had managed to smuggle
agents into British POW camps inside Germany and were in

contact with them by radio and by secret messages concealed in their mail, the Germans had done the same. Plans had been made to arrange a mass breakout from these camps and thus cause even more confusion and terror so far to the rear.

Robert B. Merriam, a historian attached to the US Ninth Army and one of the first men to examine the whole Ardennes battle from January 1945 to midsummer 1946 on the spot, had access to all records and to the highest commanders, including Eisenhower. He wrote in 1946:*

> Still another aspect of the Germans' thorough plans was the amazing scheme, somehow transmitted to Britain, for a break by all German prisoners of war. By all odds the most Wellsian phase of the German war of nerves, it has still not been completely explained. We do know that German prisoners began organizing for a mass break; that they plotted to seize arsenals, obtain tanks and actually prepare the way for German landings in England. The original date set for this break was December 16th. All this we learned from agents among the German prisoners.

And so it went on, all over Western Europe in half-a-dozen Allied countries, fuelled by ever more 'sightings' of Skorzeny's killers – and the fact that von der Heydte's paras were still at large, terrorising the snowbound countryside of the *Hohes Venn* in that remote part of Belgium, just behind the front.

3

By noon on 18 December, hours after the Big Flap had started, Baron von der Heydte established a base camp in the middle of a fir forest and began to make decisions. By now he had been joined by Lieutenant Kayser with another 150 men, making his total force 300.

Kayser was feeling full of his mission. He wanted to find the

---

* *Dark December*, published in 1947

Americans and attack immediately, especially as the convoys from the 1st, 7th and 30th American Divisions were still rolling by on the main highway, completely unaware of the paras.

Von der Heydte was more realistic. 'Attack . . . with three hundred men', he said cynically, 'and no heavy weapons?' He shook his head.

All the same Baron von der Heydte was a professional soldier who did not give in easily, in spite of the lack of men and heavy weapons and of the dreadful weather conditions. Now he took stock of his situation and equipment. After a prolonged search, a radio had been found, which didn't work, plus one heavy machine gun and a mortar, though again there was an inadequate supply of ammunition for both weapons. He concluded that the fire power of his 300 men, armed only with hand weapons, was virtually nil. So he would have to limit himself to hit-and-run tactics.

It was a decision which, unknown to von der Heydte at the time, gave his skeleton force more importance than would have resulted from their original role of holding the crossroads. For the appearance of his paras here, there and everywhere over the next few days would add immensely to the Big Flap and keep the whole front on a permanent para alert (even as far as the 1st Canadian Army a hundred miles away in Holland) till right after Christmas. For the next few days until he finally surrendered, the von der Heydte force would be searched for by thousands of American soldiers badly needed elsewhere.

Now von der Heydte sent out far-ranging patrols, as far away as Werbomont, where Peiper hoped to reach the motor highway which would take him to Huy, and, some say, even to the outskirts of Liège itself. All the time, they ambushed small American units, taking prisoners who, after being stripped of weapons and food, were sent back to their units. Naturally these badly frightened men told highly coloured tales of their experiences. Civilians were captured, too, and similarly released to add their contributions to the general atmosphere of nerves and jitters. Now once again, the long refugee columns, laden with their pathetic bits and pieces on farm carts, wheel-barrows, perambulators, anything on whccls, startcd to trudge from the Walloon-speaking areas* along the frontier, to the safety of the rear, further complicating the American supply position.

For three long, miserable days von der Heydte held out, fighting and running, fighting and running, wandering around the area enclosed by the steep-sided valleys of the Soor and Helle, which formed natural obstacles. Twice his force captured dispatch riders from General Gerow's Vth Corps Headquarters at Eupen, and volunteers were sent off with the important papers their pouches contained to attempt to reach the German lines. None of them managed to get through.

Still there was no sign of the promised link-up with Dietrich's Sixth SS. In all their days of wandering behind American lines, they made only one contact with their own forces – in the shape of a lone Junkers 88 which dropped *Essenbomben*, long, torpedo-shaped, wooden food containers. But the 'food-bombs', as the Germans called them, were a disappointment. Instead of food, the weary, exhausted paras found bottles of cheap German cognac and damp, limp cigarettes.

This discovery took the heart out of them, and by now even von der Heydte had had enough. Now the Baron felt he had only one duty: to lead his men back to safety. They had harassed the Amis as well as they could; they had done all they were able to. Now they were no longer in a position to stop the Ami convoys rolling ceaselessly southwards.†

At dawn on 21 December, the 300 paras started to move to the east. Their breath fogged on the icy air, their boots sank deep into the new snow. They crossed the first obstacle, the River Helle, fording it with the water up to their chests at a spot where a little stream called 'Good Luck'‡ flows into it. But the name was no favourable omen for them.

---

* In the complicated linguistic geography of Belgium, especially near the border, there are to be found patches of Flemish- and Walloon-speakers (French) within the predominantly German-speaking community.

† Calvin Boykin, who was in one of the 7th Armoured Division's convoys taking that road, said that he and his comrades felt that they were being 'shadowed' by German planes all the while and that there were constant airborne alerts the long, freezing journey southwards.

‡ Ruisseau de Petit Bonheur' in French

Beyond there were the heights, which were now held by the Americans. Almost immediately a fire-fight commenced. It was a brief, hot skirmish, which cost von der Heydte several men seriously wounded. The paras reeled back into cover. But in spite of his overwhelming fatigue, von der Heydte reacted. He sent out patrols to attempt to find a way through the American-held heights which barred further progress. In vain. The infantry of the 'Big Red One', America's premier infantry division, seemed to be waiting for him everywhere. More than once he attempted to make his way through fire-breaks, but each time he was stopped by a waiting Sherman tank or a Staghound armoured car.

Now von der Heydte started to break. Mistakenly believing that he was faced by men of General Maxwell Taylor's 101st Airborne Division against whom he had fought in Normandy during the invasion, he wrote a note in English to Taylor:

> We fought each other in Normandy near Carentan and from this time, I know you as a chivalrous, gallant general. I am sending you back the prisoners I took. They fought gallantly too, and I cannot care for them. . . . I am also sending you my wounded. I should greatly appreciate it, if you would give them the medical aid they need.

That done, von der Heydte left the note with his wounded and his remaining American prisoners and ordered his paras to break into groups of not more than three men. This way, he felt, they might have a chance of breaking through the Americans and escaping back to their own lines.

He let his men move out in their groups, then took off himself, accompanied only by his adjutant and his orderly, making for the picturesque little Eifel township of Monschau, just across the border which he believed (wrongly) was now back in German hands. For hours the three men wandered through those snow-bound lonely forests, heading steadily eastwards, ragged, starving and shivering in that bitter wind which always blows on those heights, even in summer.

Once they bumped into a group of his men. They wanted to join up with the Baron, believing that his superior experience would save them from captivity. Wearily von der Heydte waved them away, croaking, 'Each man must try his own luck at getting through.' They vanished, and the three stumbled on through the deep snow.

In the cold grey light of dawn the three came from the heights in Belgium and saw before them the jagged outline of Monschau's ninth-century, ruined castle below. Von der Heydte, who hadn't eaten since he had left Germany in what seemed another age, save for his iron ration, said hoarsely, 'I'm going straight to Monschau.' His arm ached agonisingly, he was starving and he thought he had frost-bitten feet; he had to find somewhere warm to rest.

The others protested. First they should scout the place out. But von der Heydte would have none of it. Instead, he bade them farewell and staggered on by himself.

Painfully he knocked at the door of the first house. There was no answer save the dull echo of his knock. It was the same at the next house, a half-timbered structure perched on a rocky outcrop from the steep hill which rises inside the little township. At the third house he was lucky. The householder, Herr Bouschery, a school-teacher, guided the exhausted Colonel gently into his warm kitchen. Gratefully von der Heydte sank down on a chair, and was told almost immediately that he was out of luck. Monschau was still firmly in American hands! Von der Heydte sank into an exhausted sleep.

Next morning, he asked for pen and paper and laboriously wrote a few lines to the American authorities, while the schoolteacher's son, Eugen Bouschery, examined his paratroop gear and told von der Heydte, 'I'm a Hitler Youth.'

But the Baron had no time for the youngster's admiration now. He was ready to throw in the sponge. He wrote that he had expected to find German troops in Monschau, but had been disappointed. Now he was confined to his bed; could he request the American commandant to send an ambulance for him? He wished to surrender! He signed the note 'Freiherr von der Heydte'.

The message caused a minor sensation at the American HQ. A German paratroop colonel and an aristocrat, to boot, right under their very noses! Immediately the two senior US officers, Captain Goetcheus and First Lieutenant Langland, set off in a jeep and an ambulance to collect von der Heydte. At the same time a anti-airborne alert was sounded, and the streets of the little place, once a favourite resort for German honeymooners, swarmed with soldiers looking for German paratroopers.

That day, as von der Heydte was taken away for treatment and interrogation, every household in Monschau was thoroughly searched for paras, and thus right to the end von der Heydte contributed to the Big Flap.

Gratefully, General Strong announced his capture at 1200 hours on 23 December stating that von der Heydte had frost-bitten feet and was suffering from incipient pneumonia. Now at last they had the man whose paras had kept the whole front line in a state of uproar and tension ever since the German offensive had started, under lock and key. Perhaps now there would be an end to the Big Flap?

But Kenneth Strong's calculations were wrong. The first of the three colonels had, indeed, 'gone into the bag', and the second, as yet unknown to Eisenhower's Chief-of-Intelligence, was sitting out the battle in the comfort of his HQ in far-off Bonn. However, there was still the third. Now it was the turn of Obersturmbannführer Otto Skorzeny, the most 'dangerous man in Europe', as the US press was by this time calling him, to take the stage, only a matter of miles away from where von der Heydte was holding his first US press conference for the benefit of a bunch of eager US war correspondents, who knew that they had been boring their readers with stories of waiting around in the snow.* Operation 'Trojan Horse' could now commence.

---

*They made von der Heydte out to be some sort of film hero: a para colonel, aristocrat and anti-Nazi to boot. He even had a 'favourite sport'. At the conference someone asked him what he thought of Sepp Dietrich. Was he a great strategist? Now von der Heydte had his revenge for the 'pigeons'. He snarled, 'He is a cur dog!' The remark went the rounds of the world's press.

THREE
Operation 'Trojan Horse'

1

On the day that von der Heydte surrendered to the Americans at Monschau, some 30 miles away Obersturmbann-führer Jochen Peiper found himself with what was left of his Kampfgruppe bottled up in the hilltop hamlet of La Gleize.

La Gleize – a church, a school, a vicarage, a tavern and a handful of houses – was some 4 miles away from Werbomont where Peiper had hoped to take the motor road directly to Huy. Now his 3,000-odd men were crammed into the hamlet and outskirts, surrounded by elements of three US divisions – the 82nd, the 30th and the 3rd Armoured – and their position was becoming more desperate by the hour.

Already the village was under direct American fire from 155mm cannon, and Peiper's supplies of fuel, ammunition and medicines were running out rapidly, as the cellars started to fill with ever more German wounded.

For forty-eight hours the 1st SS Corps, commanded by bullet-headed General Priess, who had successfully held Metz against Patton for three months in the autumn, tried to reach Peiper. But the Americans holding the river line east of La Gleize threw back all attempts to cross, with heavy German casualties. All that Priess was able to do was to air-drop petrol to the trapped commander and float some more down the rivers. Skorzeny's supply officer had managed to infiltrate a few vehicles laden with supplies, too. Priess knew that Peiper couldn't hold out much longer; he had to be relieved – and relieved soon.

Now a disturbing message was received at the headquarters of the 1st SS Panzer Division, to which Peiper belonged; it was simple and direct. 'Almost all our Hermann* is gone. We have no Otto.† It's just a question of time before we're completely destroyed. *Can we break out?*'

The degree of Peiper's desperation was evidenced by the fact he had sent the message in clear for any listening Ami to pick up.

Priess, who thought that Peiper was being sacrificed unnecessarily, was forced to turn the request down. The Führer himself had rejected it. He still believed that Peiper, if reinforced, could reach that vital bridge at Huy. Thus it was that Priess called up all his reserves, including Otto Skorzeny's Panzerbrigade 150, for a determined attack with the purpose of breaking the American stranglehold and reaching Peiper.

Skorzeny's objective was the key town of Malmédy, from which the winding mountain road led to La Gleize. In theory, Skorzeny's soldiers would be committed in a conventional infantry–armoured role; in practice, Skorzeny was not going to waste all that training in unconventional warfare. If it were at all possible, his was going to be a Trojan Horse operation. For already he had several times had men in and out of the town without discovery. If a few pseudo-Americans could do it, then his camouflaged Panthers and handful of Shermans could do the same and lead the way for a surprise attack by his whole Brigade. Hadn't Troy been captured by a similar trick? This time the horse wouldn't be of wood, but of good, solid Krupp steel!

Lieutenant-Commander von Beer, an elderly naval officer now disguised as a somewhat unlikely American lieutenant, was the first jeep-team commander to enter Malmédy. However as he commented drily to Skorzeny later, 'I crossed

---

* Ammunition
† Petrol

the front line by mistake. It wouldn't have happened to me at sea, believe you me, Obersturmbannführer.'

He had ridden around the medieval town to find it virtually empty of Amis. He had been stopped, but by Belgian civilians, who asked him fearfully, 'Are the Germans coming back?' Von Beer replied truthfully that he didn't know, and fled back the way he had come. Later he remarked, 'We got away with it that time because we had more luck than sense.'

But Lieutenant Commander von Beer was not the only pseudo-American who had penetrated the Malmédy area that Sunday.

On the same day, Sergeant Keogan of the 291st Engineers, which would bear the brunt of the Skorzeny 'Trojan Horse' operation at Malmédy, was working on detached duty on the road that led from the town to Eupen when he came across a massive traffic jam with angry MPs trying to sort it out. It was a snarled-up convoy of the 1st Division's 16th Regiment.

One of the MPs told Keogan, 'We had some boys going down where that breakthrough's at, and some damned jokers changed the road signs. They sent the whole outfit on west down the wrong road! When we got on the trail of it there was two of 'em still standing out here in the road turning 'em wrong!'

Puzzled, Sergeant Keogan asked who had changed the road signs. '*Krauts!*' an irate MP snapped. 'In an American uniform, too. They had a jeep, and when we got here they jumped in and made off so fast one of 'em was still standing on the front bumper hanging on to wire clippers. They hauled out of here going fifty miles an hour!'

Keogan laughed at the look of frustrated anger on the MP's face, but then he got thinking and decided he had better report back. With Germans dressed as American GIs, spying, changing road signs, perhaps even committing acts of sabotage, the open road was no place to be this icy December day.

For the first time the Americans at Malmédy had some indication that all was not well. Malmédy no longer looked the picture-book town, straight out of Hansel and Gretel, that they had first imagined it to be; a decent place to be stationed after the dreary, dull hamlets of the Ardennes. They looked at the local civilians with different eyes, sensing, or so they thought, a strong pro-German and anti-American feeling coming from them. They felt the locals were already spying on them, ready to betray them to the Germans at the drop of a hat. Now the rumour was that the Germans already had secret control of Malmédy and could come and go as they wished, helped by their sympathisers and the many refugees who were of German stock now inside its boundaries.

Already there was talk that an agent within Malmédy had directed the fire of the big German cannon on the first day of the attack. Now came Keogan's tale, to be followed a day later by the report from the engineers manning a road-block outside the town that their positions had been betrayed to a probing German patrol by a housewife.

Suddenly an air of mystery and fear hung over the little town in the valley. It seemed an unhappy place, as if it was destined to suffer some dreadful fate. How right the nervous engineers were, they little knew, on that Sunday, 17 December, 1944.

It was one o'clock in the afternoon when it all started. At the Café Bodarwé, which is located on the heights above Malmédy at the crossroads (that branch off to St Vith and Büllingen), local farmer Henri le Joly was standing in the kitchen talking to Madame Bodarwé, whose son was serving in the German army, when an American jeep stopped.

An officer got out, and asked in French, '*Avez-vous vu les Allemands?*'

Le Joly shrugged, and pretended he couldn't speak French. He made no secret of his pro-German feeling; he had, after all, been born a German.

The American muttered something, and prepared to rejoin the convoy from Battery B, 285th Field Artillery Observation Battalion. This was a green outfit as yet unattached to any corps or division, and it was to achieve greater glory in the manner of its death than it had ever done in its life.

At that moment, the first half-track of Peiper's Kampfgruppe, barrelling westwards, came rattling round the corner. The Germans began firing at once. An American truck went up in flames. A jeep careened into a ditch. In an instant, the

Americans were fleeing from their trucks, trying to find cover anywhere they could.

The skirmish didn't last long. Almost immediately the Americans started to raise their hands, and Madame Bodarwé's kitchen was filled with mud-splattered Panzer grenadiers in camouflaged suits, looking for food and drink.

Peiper himself raced round the corner in his Volkswagen jeep intent on reaching the next village, Ligneuville, where, it was rumoured, an American general had his headquarters – and Peiper had never captured an American general before. He wanted to add him to the sundry Greek, Yugoslav, French and Russian generals he had already captured in his long fighting career.

Le Joly sensed that there was trouble to come. The guards left to watch the 100-odd American prisoners were in an excited, vengeful mood. According to them, an American prisoner back at Büllingen had escaped by killing one of their comrades with a pocket-knife. Glad as he was to see his former countrymen back in the east cantons, Le Joly was worried about what they might do.

As the first wave of Peiper's Kampfgruppe disappeared down the hill which led to Ligneuville, two armoured vehicles stopped directly in front of the prisoners lined up in the field next to Café Bodarwé. In one of them, commanded by Sergeant Hans Siptrott, Private Georg Fleps, a native Romanian-German, pulled out his pistol and took careful aim.

He fired, his reason for doing so unclear to this day.* He couldn't miss. Among them was Second Lieutenant Virgil Lary, whose driver groaned out loud and, clutching his chest, fell to the ground.

'*Stand fast!*' Lary cried.

Too late. Now more and more Germans began to join in. At the door of the café, Le Joly watched in horror, as the prisoners started to fall in groups. A machine gun opened up. The survivors broke ranks and tried to make a run for it. Most of them didn't make it. They were cut down as they fled.

Some of the Americans dropped automatically, hit or not.

---

* Revealed in conversation with the author

Homer D. Ford, a military policeman was one. Sergeant Ken Ahrens was another, as also was Samuel Dobyns, a medic who had been recommended for saving German wounded under fire in Normandy. Perhaps twenty men in all, lay among the dead and dying waiting for the firing to stop so that they could escape. But it looked as if there were going to be no survivors of the Malmédy Massacre. As the survivors told it later, the Germans waded through the ranks of the dead, kicking each one and, if he grunted in pain, finishing him off with a pistol shot to the back of the skull. As they did so, they laughed out loud.

'Maniacal,' was Lieutenant Lary's description of the sound many years laters.

Samuel Dobyns decided to make a run for it before it was too late. Suddenly he was up and pelting for the woods beyond the café. A machine gun opened up. Dobyns yelled. Four slugs slammed into his body. Eight others ripped his uniform to shreds. He hit the ground hard. Three SS men started to come towards him to finish him off. But abruptly they changed their minds and turned. Perhaps they thought the Ami was dead already. Dobyns didn't know or care. He felt that he was dying anyway.

At last the Germans were about spent. Le Joly fled. They were coming towards the café. He shouted for Madame Bodarwé to run into the cellar, and then pelted across the road to his own farm. That was the last that was ever seen of Madame Bodarwé. Soon her café was burning fiercely and she was gone.* Half an hour later the SS were gone, continuing their drive which would take them to that trap in the village of La Gleize.

Sergeant Ahrens, who had been wounded twice in the back, staggered to his feet and began to head down the steep descent into Malmédy, bleeding heavily. Lieutenant Lary was also alive. A bullet had severed his toes and the pain was terrific, but still he was alive and could move. All around him he could hear frightened whispers, 'Have they gone? . . .

---

*Buried in the rubble after the war, her son Louis found a severed woman's leg. It could have been that of his mother, he thought.

Is it safe? . . . What shall we do? . . . What about the wounded?'

Some fifteen to twenty men levered themselves up. There seemed to be no Germans about. They started to run. Rifle fire broke the tense silence. They scattered wildly. Some headed for a house, but a machine gun spat fire from it. They fell or fled.

Lary clambered over a fence and ran along a dirt road until he came to a tumble-down shack. Hurriedly he hid behind a pile of logs, his boot full of blood.

Ahrens hobbled into a wood. In the trees he tried to catch his breath. But he knew he couldn't stop there. The Germans would find him and this time he wouldn't escape. Summoning up the last of his strength, dribbling blood, he staggered on towards the little town in the valley below whose name would soon signify to the Western world one thing only – massacre!*

2

Lieutenant-Colonel Pergrim, the dark-haired, bespectacled CO of 291st Combat Engineers, was one of the first to encounter the survivors. He had just been informed that an American jeep with Germans in American uniform had hit the mines at one of his command's road-blocks, killing all four Germans, leaving the tyres from the wrecked jeep hanging from trees 30 feet above the ground. Now fire was reported from the crossroads above Malmédy.

Taking with him Sergeant Crickenberger, he drove forward to reconnoitre, moving to the high ground above 'Five Corners' (as the crossroads were called by the GIs), and then went ahead on foot.

When he reached the woods, he reported later, 'three

---

*What happened at that crossroads resulted in a trial which involved archbishops, senators and even President Eisenhower. Peiper took the blame on himself for what had happened there and was sentenced to death. Major Poetschke, in charge (who was, incidentally, born in Belgium) was killed before the end of the war. As Peiper said to the author, 'No one will ever know the truth of what happened there.'

American soldiers came limping out screaming incoherently. One of them was a lieutenant who had been wounded in the heel.' This was Lary, who was taken back to the battalion aid station, where later he was joined by seventeen other survivors.

Just as the first group arrived there for treatment, two war correspondents, Hal Boyle and Jack Belden of *Time Magazine*, drove up and made the scoop of their careers. They listened in silence while the survivors, 'half-frozen, dazed, weeping with anger', told their tales. Lieutenant Lary told his story while he shook the bloody remains of his toes out of his shoe, sobbing, *'We didn't have a chance!'*

The effect of the survivors' stories, on top of the already tense atmosphere at Malmédy, can be imagined. As far as the engineers knew, the enemy was on both flanks and to their rear (Peiper's men). Not only that, there was an active fifth column, so they thought, inside the town itself. And their fate, if captured, was obvious; they would be gunned down in cold blood just as the artillerymen had been at 'Five Corners'.

To bolster the defence force some infantry from the 30th Infantry Division, in addition to a Norwegian service battalion, normally employed in cutting timber, entered Malmédy. As darkness fell, the waiting infantry, engineers and lumberjacks hugged the protection of their holes. Now it took a brave man to move from one outpost to another, as the defenders were inclined to shoot first and ask questions afterwards. That night the Americans shot two of their own men dead thinking they were Germans, and the word was passed from post to post, as the news of the tragic accident made its rounds, 'For God's sake, be careful!'

On the following day one of Skorzeny's men, dressed in American uniform, was captured. He was taken to the headquarters of the 120th Infantry Regiment and 'interrogated all night'. He told, in particular, what the morrow would bring for the defenders of Malmédy. From the village of Bütgenbach to Malmédy itself, there was going to be an all-out attack by the 1st SS Panzer Corps. Dietrich had ordered a final massive attempt to break through to Peiper. Malmédy itself would be attacked by his own unit, the 150 Panzer brigade at 3:30 a.m., although how, he didn't know.

Immediately the three colonels now commanding in Malmédy were told and they, in their turn, alerted their men. By
just after twelve on the morning of Thursday, 21 December,
the mixed force of engineers, lumberjacks and infantry were
in position and waiting. The question was now, how and
where would the attack come?

Leutnant Peter Mandt, now disguised as a corporal in the US
army, moved into his jump-off position with the Panzerbrigade just before midnight, with his Panther tank crudely
altered to look something like an American one. Mandt had
spent years as a tank commander on the Russian front before
volunteering for Skorzeny's clandestine outfit, and was not
particularly worried about the action to come.

'We knew we were going to lose the war anyway,' he
recorded much later,' and regarded battle as a kind of gigantic
lottery, with the big prize – survival.'

Now Mandt's Panther rolled into its position on the
Falize road, where it would be part of the left prong of
Skorzeny's 'Trojan Horse' attack, while the right prong went
in from the heights at Baugnez, the notorious 'Five Corners'.
Here, unknown to Skorzeny's men, the bodies of the victims
of the Malmédy Massacre were frozen solid beneath the sheet
of new snow, near the ruins of Café Bodarwé.

The Panther halted 100 yards away from the railway
viaduct at Malmédy, still undetected by the handful of Amis
holding the place, and Mandt ordered his radioman to tune to
the soldiers' favourite propaganda station, *Soldatensender
Calais*. The supposed German station was always good for the
latest German records and some scurrilous tales about the
goings-on, back home, of the 'Golden Pheasants', as the
ordinary soldiers contemptuously named Party officials because of their love of gold braid and decorations.

However, tonight the British station, commanded by that
master of black propaganda, ex-*Daily Express* chief reporter
Sefton Delmer, had something more serious and very alarm-
ing to report to his listeners waiting to go into the attack.
Suddenly the music stopped. A harsh voice barked above the
sounds of someone calling out commands in English, followed a second later by a sharp volley of musketry, '*Mit diesen*

Salven endete ein weiteres Einsatzkommando Skorzenya!'
('With these volleys another one of Skorzeny's commando-
teams met its end').*

The radioman switched off the set hurriedly, and the men
huddled in the green gloom of the tank stared at each with
shocked faces. Mandt and his men were fatalists all right, but
they wanted to give themselves a chance, at least. *They
weren't going to be shot out of hand as spies if they were
captured in the battle to come.* Hurriedly, they started to strip
off their American uniforms and replace them with German
parachutist gear.

At 3.30 a.m. precisely, as the prisoner had revealed, the
attack began. From Bütgenbach to Malmédy, Dietrich's SS
made a last desperate attempt to break through to Peiper at
La Gleize. From two directions, Skorzeny's disguised tanks
came in, with infantry covering them in the fields to both
sides.

Almost immediately they ran into trouble. The engineers
had strung trip-wires across the fields, attached to flares.
Skorzeny's men stumbled right into them, and at once flares
were hissing into the night sky on all sides, to explode and
colour their shocked faces glowing icy white.

Close to the point on the Falize road, Mandt and his crew
hastily got rid of their 'American camouflage' and rattled to
the attack. 'Night seemed to have been turned into day,' he
recorded later. 'Christmas trees'† were coming down on all
sides, and already the American anti-tank cannon were bark-
ing. Solid armour-piercing shells were hurrying towards us
like glowing golf balls.'

T/5 Vincent Consiglio, Privates Mitchell and Spires of the
Engineers, all armed with rifles, saw the lead tanks coming
down the road, going all out. They decided they couldn't do
anything against them with their rifles. They fled. A house

---

*This was probably faked. The first of Skorzeny's commandos weren't
shot, as we shall see, till thirty-six hours later. By this time *Soldatensender
Calais* had reported 250 Skorzeny commandos captured, although there
were only 200 in the whole unit.

† German soldier's slang for multiple flares

loomed up out of the glowing white gloom. It was occupied by a platoon of the 823rd Tank Destroyer Battalion. The three engineers were quickly assigned look-out posts, Consiglio being given the basement.

He broke the little window and peered out. Only yards away there was a steel monster, decorated with the white star of the Allied force, but it was German all right and its big gun was swinging round like the trunk of some primeval monster sniffing out its prey. Almost immediately the Panther's 75mm. cannon thundered. Consiglio was knocked off his feet by the blast. Recovering, he staggered upstairs.

The house was a smoking, shattered shambles. All the anti-tank men had been killed outright. Blindly Consiglio stumbled through the wreckage, and bumped into Mitchell, who had found a bazooka.

'Help me get into this gear,' Mitchell snarled. 'I'm gonna get that bastard!'

The next moment a machine gun opened up close by. Slugs sprayed the house, and plaster and brick flew everywhere. Mitchell yelled and fell headfirst out of the window, killed instantly. The tank rumbled on, leaving behind a house full of dead men and one crazy engineer.

Leutnant Mandt had just reached the outskirsts of Malmédy when it happened. The 50-ton Panther was 'rocked as if by a steel fist': Mandt's tank had just been hit by the Allies' new secret weapon, the POZIT fuse, a shell which exploded not on impact but by proximity to its target. Groggily, Mandt and two survivors staggered from the wrecked Panther, leaving two dead men behind, and crawled to the safety of the Café Lodomez, where one of Skorzeny's 'Shermans' had skidded on the slippery road and crashed right into the kitchen, the long cannon of the disguised Panther resting a yard above the cooking stove (where it remained as a macabre souvenir of Operation 'Trojan Horse' till the summer of 1947). Now Skorzeny's tanks were really running into trouble. Consiglio, still alone with the dead, saw a German tank receive a direct hit on the wooden bridge down below. Its crew baled out frantically and pelted to a nearby ditch. One by one they were flushed out by the American infantry, swarming forward to meet the attack until there was only one of them left, running right down the middle of the road. Consiglio had no mercy after what he had just experienced. He pressed the trigger of his rifle. The butt slammed into his shoulder. The German crumpled to the ground, dead.

Skorzeny's attack from the right was meeting with no better success. Here, too, the Americans, a mixed bunch of infantry and engineers, were waiting for them. The first German half-track rolling down from 'Five Corners' ran straight into the daisy-chain of mines the engineers had stretched across the road. It went up in a mad roar, flinging its dead and dying crew high into the skeletal trees on both sides of the winding road. All of them were wearing American uniform. One took a long time dying, lying in the road, screaming with the agony of his burns. No one took pity on him.

Now the artillery cracked into action. The advancing Germans were plastered and soon started to surrender. The first to come in, also dressed in American uniform, was a former ballet manager, who had taken his troupe to the States before the war. He told his captors confidently in excellent English, 'You can never win the war. We have so many new secret weapons.'

It is possible that he ended his career dancing on the end of a rope, like so many others of Skorzeny's 'Trojan Horse' Operation, for having worn American uniform in action.

Another group approached, driving in a captured US M-8 scout car. It, too, ran into the minefield just after it left 'Five Corners'. Madly the Germans scrambled for cover in a house next to Henri le Joly's farm. They did not stay there for long. In the eerie pink light of the battle, three of the Germans made a run for a jeep, which had been abandoned close by. It started immediately, and they raced towards the wrecked half-track in a bold attempt to rescue the man dying of burns.

One of the engineers challenged them. In heavily accented English, one of the men in the jeep cried out, 'You're crazy!', as another attempted to drag the wounded man inside. Again the Americans at the road-block showed no mercy. They poured a withering volley of machine-gun and bazooka fire at the stationary jeep. It went up in the air, as had the half-track and the scout car. Two of its occupants were killed outright. The other was captured.

Now, in spite of the terrifying weight of artillery shells, directed by the new top secret fuse, which were descending upon them, Skorzeny's men pressed home their attack boldly, shouting in English as they raced across the snowy fields in waves, 'Surrender or die!'

But this time it was the Germans who were dying. Leutnant Mandt had been ordered forward again to take command of a group of infantry, but as he closed up to them, he discovered that they were no longer so eager. The cellars of the houses in which they were hiding were filled with wounded, and two noncoms to whom he spoke said it was certain death to raise one's head up into the open.

Mandt, however, knew that, as an officer, he couldn't stay cowering in the cellar. 'I crawled out therefore and started collecting the few surviving infantry to renew the attack.' But he was soon relieved of the need to make a decision:

'Suddenly I felt a blow on my head, as if from a hammer. I lost consciousness. When I came to again, after how long I don't know, I found my head soaked in blood and that I was lying between two men to whom I had been speaking when I had been hit. They were both very dead!'

The Germans were being slaughtered by the score as they reached the embankment of the railway line that ran to the west of Malmédy. Desperately they went to ground and tried to set up their machine guns. The Americans didn't give them a chance. They swamped the embankment with artillery shells. For two solid hours they pounded it, stopping the Germans in their tracks. Yet the Germans would not give up, and fought on desperately, clinging tenaciously to their positions on the embankment, the wooden bridge, and the paper mill.

At the bridge, the twelve Americans left at Consiglio's house out of the thirty-three who had originally moved in to defend it after the anti-tank men had been wiped out, were running out of ammunition.

Consiglio volunteered to go and fetch help with one of the

infantrymen, although they were told, 'You're a dead duck the minute you stick your nose out of this house.'

Outside, the two of them put a full clip into their rifles and then stripped off their heavy equipment. Then Consiglio started running. 'I never ran as hard or as fast in my life,' he recalled after the war. 'I really had wings on my feet. You never know how fast you can go until you've got bullets nipping at your heels.'

He and the unknown infantryman made it, only to run into trouble from their own side.

'Halt!' someone shouted in the darkness. For some reason a winded Consiglio blurted out the first word that came into his head. To his horror it was the German term for surrender: *'Kamerad!'*

Things happened fast after that. The Americans at the machine-gun post thought that they had captured two Germans posing as Americans. They jumped on the two escapees, gave them a couple of nasty slaps and stood them up against a wall, as if they were going to be shot there and then. Fortunately, just then a captain came up who recognised Consiglio's companion, and they were saved. But when the engineer was sent on to a higher headquarters to ask for reinforcements for the hard-pressed men at the wooden bridge he realised that his capture as a suspected German agent was symptomatic of the current state of American morale. The officers here seemed to him totally confused, believing that Skorzeny's men in American uniform had broken through their lines everywhere and were roaming around at will. No reinforcements were sent.

In reality, it was all over bar the shouting. All Skorzeny's disguised tanks had been destroyed, captured or otherwise put out of action, and although his men were still clinging to the positions captured, they were making no further progress.

That dawn on the ridge overlooking Malmédy, now wreathed in smoke, stabbed here and there by the cherry-red of shells exploding, Skorzeny watched as the first beaten infantrymen came streaming back, half in American, half in German uniform. Among them was young, blond Hauptsturmbannführer von Foelkersam, one of the bravest of his commanders. They laughed together as the young man explained he had been shot in the rump, but Skorzeny could see the exhaustion and disappointment on his face. Although von Foelkersam wanted to continue the fight, Skorzeny ordered a general withdrawal up to the hilltop. Operation 'Trojan Horse' had been a failure.

As the defeated stragglers and the half-tracks filled with wounded started to withdraw round 'Five Corners', Skorzeny himself made his way to his HQ at nearby Ligneuville.

Just outside the Hôtel du Moulin, he heard the howl of shells coming over from Malmédy. Too late: just as he attempted to take cover, a shell exploded nearby. Skorzeny staggered violently, blood jetting from a wound on his face. He had been hit.

A soldier ran to help him. He waved him away. He stumbled into the hotel and demanded a cognac. He got one from the stock of the US general who had fled before Peiper had been able to capture him. Downing it in one gulp, Skorzeny looked at himself in the mirror. 'I felt the blood running warmly down my cheek,' he recorded later. 'Carefully I felt my face with my hand. Above my eye a lump of flesh was hanging from my forehead. I was shocked. Was my eye gone?'

It wasn't.

A little later Skorzeny was operated on without benefit of anaesthetics because he wanted to keep a clear head. The doctor probed with his instruments while Skorzeny bit his teeth together as he had done in the days of his youth after a student duel. But the wound was clear, and finally Skorzeny was released after the hole had been sewn up, his head bound in a thick bandage, temporarily blind in one eye.

Six days later his Brigade was relieved by an infantry division and was withdrawn to the German frontier, where Skorzeny soon left it for good – but not before an enquiry came from the High Command, asking if the 150th knew anything of an alleged massacre near Malmédy. *Soldatensender Calais* had just broadcast details of the shooting of US prisoners of war at the crossroads at Baugnez. Skorzeny replied in the negative. 'A German front-line officer would never allow a crime of that nature,' he recorded, 'and a

German front-line soldier would never dream of carrying it
out.' Otto Skorzeny was in for a shock.

3

The Americans and remaining Belgians in Malmédy were to
be shocked, too. Although they had, indeed, beaten off the
Trojan Horse operation and put Skorzeny to flight, they were
not destined to escape the fate that many of them felt hung
over the city. By the time Skorzeny's survivors had been
withdrawn to the frontier, the city would be in ashes ánd
several hundred of the defenders, as well as 220 civilians,
would be dead – killed by their own people!

The first accident happened on the morning of Saturday, 23
December. The day dawned cold, crisp and bright. The
'Führer's weather' had come to an end for a while. For the
first time since the start of the offensive, the weather was ideal
for flying.

Behind the front, from airfields in France, Luxembourg
and Belgium, Allied planes took to the air in their hundreds.
One such group was from the 322nd US Bombardment Group
of the Ninth Air Force. They were flying in a silver 'V'
escorted by fighters, to bomb their primary target, the
Rhenish city of Zülpich. Somehow, though, they couldn't find
Zülpich, so they turned to their secondary target, the small
town of Lommersum, to the south-west of Zülpich.

The lead plane zoomed ever lower. There was no flak; it
looked as if it would be easier than falling off a log. Suddenly
the intercom was full of the bombardier's triumphant, '*Bombs
away!*' The B-29 lurched as thirteen 250-lb general purpose
bombs screeched towards the enemy township. Almost immediately great mushrooms of thick black smoke began to
ascend to the hard blue winter sky. One by one the others
followed, to release their deadly eggs on the target before
swinging round in a great gleaming arc. Minutes later they
were heading for home, for debriefing and bacon and eggs.
Lommersum had been well and truly 'plastered'.

Down below the civilians and soldiers of Malmédy began to crawl out of the smoking ruins to stare with horror at the lunar landscape of what had once been a pretty little country town.

Almost immediately portly, bad-tempered General Hobbs of the 30th Division was on the phone to the Air Force. Hobbs had already had bad experiences with the Ninth Air Force; they had bombed his troops before in the Normandy fighting with many casualties. Now the 'American Luftwaffe' had killed thirty-seven men of his division, wounded a large number, and killed and wounded an unknown number of Belgian civilians.

What in Sam Hill was going on? Didn't the Air Force know that Malmédy was firmly in American hands after beating off Skorzeny's attack?

The Air Force apologised and promised it would never, *but never*, happen again! But it did: *twice more*! On Christmas Eve and once again on Christmas Day. Perhaps Air Force General Quesada's men took a particular pleasure in bombing this place which had now become established throughout the Western world as the site of the infamous Malmédy Massacre. To destroy it would even up the score a bit, they thought possibly. No one knows today. Perhaps it was just fate. But in the end the Ninth Air Force left behind a shattered city of death, gutted by fire, abandoned by most of the citizens who had survived and even by those who had once defended it against Skorzeny. Now only stray dogs and cats, and fat, contented rats roamed the smoking streets.

The day of the bombing marked the real end of Skorzeny's unit, which had been set up so confidently that October.

On the twenty-second, General Hodges, who had fled with his headquarters – first to Chaudfontaine and then once again to the other side of the Meuse, to Tongres – had a difficult decision to make. He had to pass sentence of death on the men of Corporal Schmidt's team, who had started the great 'Eisenhower scare'. They had pleaded in a written appeal:

The personal ambition of a single man is responsible for this criminal action. We were taken out of our old units because we knew English and with the understanding that we would be interpreters. . . . Only shortly before our commitment were we informed of the criminal background of the whole enterprise. One of our comrades who refused to obey the order was court-martialled and undoubtedly sentenced to death. . . . We were captured by the Americans without having fired a shot because we didn't want to become murderers. We were sentenced to death and are now dying for some criminals who have not only us, but also – and that is worse – our families on their conscience. Therefore, we beg mercy of the Commanding General; we have not been unjustly sentenced, but we are *de facto* innocent.

But the appeal had no effect. General Hodges had already been informed verbally by General Bradley that he could pass sentence of death on the three Germans and have the sentence executed as soon as possible. Hodges realised the necessity of executing the men immediately and having the execution receive the widest possible publicity to discourage other Germans from wearing American uniforms; but he was too old a soldier to have a man executed without written authority. He asked for a decision from Bradley in writing. *

On that blue winter morning when the martyrdom of Malmedy commenced, he received it and duly passed it on to the military police authorities who were going to carry out the execution.

The execution was stage-managed carefully to achieve the fullest possible effect on morale and steadfastness – and perhaps also in a small way could be seen as a token of revenge for what had happened at 'Five Corners' six days before. The press was invited, as was a horde of photographers, and an official war artist, Sergeant Howard Bardie, to capture the Germans' last moments. Regulations were consulted on the correct manner for carrying out the execution by firing squad. In 'Preliminary Preparations', Regulation SOP No. 54 stated:

---

* On the same day, still 'imprisoned' at Versailles, Eisenhower confirmed the death sentence on Private Eddie Slovik, the only American soldier to be shot for desertion since 1865. It, and the death sentences on the Germans, showed how desperate the Allied High Command was to stop panic and maintain morale.

The place of execution will be prepared to provide for a back wall made of absorbent material, before which the prisoner will be placed. An upright post will be placed in front of the back wall and will be used to support the prisoner if necessary.

The requisite wall was found without too much difficulty, in the little village of Henri Chapelle north of Eupen. (It is still there, marred only by the marks of the bullets which did not hit their living targets.)

A firing squad was formed of military policemen, as the SOP prescribed 'in charge of a sergeant, consisting of not less than eight and not more than twelve enlisted men, skilled in the use of the regulation rifle'. Finally the personnel specified by the SOP for such an execution were selected: three medical officers, a chaplain, a recorder and not fewer than five officially designated military witnesses.

Now all was ready; the prisoners could be told.

The three of them took the news that their appeal had been turned down bravely, and they remained brave right to the end. They were asked if they had any last request, as specified in the regulations.

'Yes,' they said. 'You have some German women prisoners. We would like to hear German Christmas Carols.' The request was granted.

With the last echoes of '*Stille Nacht, Heilige Nacht*', sung by the scores of German women who had been rounded up in the great spy scare they had occasioned, still ringing in their ears, the three men were led out, tied to stakes, blindfolded and had white paper hearts pinned to their breasts just above their real hearts.

The officer in charge of the execution stepped forward and read out their sentence once again. Smartly he moved back out of range. The sergeant in command of the firing squad took over. As prescribed by the SOP, he called, '*Squad! . . . Ready! . . . Aim! . . . Fire!*'

It was all over.

Nazi Twilight

1

On the morning of 24 December 1944, German armour was still pushing hard to reach the Meuse. To the south of the Bulge, the German 2nd Armoured Division was on the road to Celles, only 5 miles from the Meuse. To the north, its namesake, the 2nd SS Armoured Division of Dietrich's Sixth SS Army, was now only 4 miles below the next junction on the vital Bastogne–Liège highway at Manhay, while Bastogne itself was surrounded, though not under attack. This made the defenders – now calling themselves 'the Battered Bastards of the Bastion of Bastogne' – very glad. For the airborne troopers of the 101st Airborne had just about reached the end of their tether. That morning their commander, General McAuliffe, told General Middleton, commander of the shattered US VIIIth Corps, 'The finest Christmas present the 101st could get would be a relief tomorrow.'

However, although the German threat was still serious and there was much hard and bitter fighting to come before the attackers were finally defeated, Dietrich and von Manteuffel knew that the steam was running out of the last offensive in the west. Talking from a *château* near the Belgian township of La Roche, not far from the Meuse, Hasso von Manteuffel, commander of the Fifth Panzer Army, ex-gentleman jockey, told General Jodl at the Führer's HQ over the phone that day 'Time is running short. Brandenberger's Seventh Army isn't far enough forward to cover my left flank. I expect a heavy Allied attack at any moment from the south. You've got to let me know this evening what the Führer wants. The time has come for a completely new plan. I can't keep driving toward the Meuse and still take Bastogne.'

'The Führer won't like this news,' Jodl, Hitler's cunning-faced Chief-of-Operations said anxiously.

'It's the damn truth', Manteuffel snapped. 'The most we can do is to reach the Meuse. We've been delayed too long at Bastogne. Anyone can see the Seventh Army is too weak to hold off a heavy attack from the south. Besides, by this time the Allies are sure to be on the other side of the Meuse in strength.'

'But the Führer will never give up the drive for Antwerp,' Jodl protested. 'Believe me.'

Von Manteuffel was unmoved. He demanded a change of plan before it was too late and in the end Jodl promised, 'Be assured, my dear Manteuffel, the Führer will be told immediately.'

And that was that. Von Manteuffel hung up as Allied shells started to pound the *château*. He hurried to the cellar to join the rest of his staff sheltering there. Their pale, unshaven faces told him all he wanted to know: the offensive had failed. Now it would become a matter of trying to pick up the pieces.

The man who was leading that drive from the south to relieve Bastogne was General Patton. He had gone into the battle five days before, stating, 'Everyone in this Army must understand that we are not fighting this battle in any half-cocked manner. Shoot the works! If those Hun bastards can do it that way, so can we.'

Now on the twenty-fourth, with his beloved 4th Armoured Division fully committed to battling their way through a dozen Belgian villages held by a German parachute division, his mood was not so ebullient. He had promised Eisenhower the relief of Bastogne by Christmas, and with only hours to go, the 4th were now stuck at a railway line far from the besieged town, and the two infantry divisions flanking them were doing no better.

'The advances for the day were not impressive, varying from two to five miles,' he wrote in his diary moodily, and his frame of mind was not helped by the fact that his command post kept receiving messages from the 'Battered Bastards' which hinted that the Fourth Armoured should get a move on.

General McAuliffe radioed,

'Sorry I didn't get to shake hands today. I was disappointed.'

One of the airborne staff was less formal. He radioed the headquarters of the 4th that midnight: 'There is only one more shopping day before Christmas!'

Everywhere this last Christmas Eve of the war the front was settling down. Back in London, the seriousness of the struggle in the Ardennes was revealed by the *Daily Mail*, which complained that 'there is not enough beer in some parts of the country to last over the holidays. . . . Many public houses may have to shut down on Christmas Day.'

As always the English took their pleasures decidedly sadly. Paris, closer to the front, was still gripped by a spy scare. There were reports of lynchings. An army of fifth columnists was ready, so it was recorded, to rise from the sewers at a moment's notice. At Supreme Headquarters they had 'baited the hook' for Skorzeny. Colonel Baldwin B. Smith, Ike's double, was openly riding back and forth between the Supreme Commander's home and Versailles, just waiting for 'the most dangerous man in Europe' to take a shot at him.

In fact, there was not a Skorzeny 'killer' within miles of Paris, though, reportedly, several score of suspects went to join the 1,308 American officers and enlisted men already in the Paris stockade, half of them there on charges of stealing from their comrades to sell on the European black market.

As Colonel E. G. Buhrmaster, Provost Marshal of the Seine Base Section, commented angrily, 'This place is getting to be like Chicago in the days of Al Capone. They hijack trucks right off the road. One major sent home $36,000 in a few weeks!' Thus the 'suspects', probably harmless GIs themselves, spent Christmas Eve among the worst kind of army crooks: rear-echelon troops who robbed their fighting comrades at the front. If bullets had had any saleable value, undoubtedly they would have sold them too.

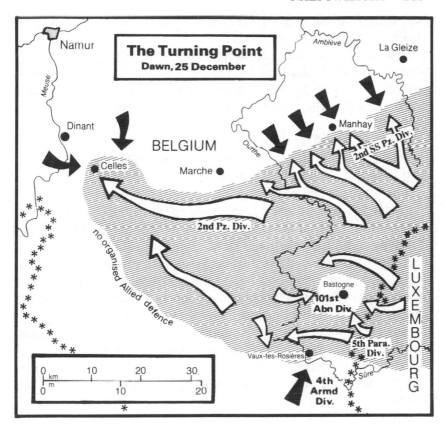

As night descended upon war-torn Europe, it brought with it a strange kind of respite from the bloody struggles of the day and the new ones of the morrow. In Malmédy, the exhausted men of the 291st Engineers celebrated with one bottle of champagne poured into tin cups around a Christmas tree which was decorated with photographs of their loved ones back home in lieu of gifts; they had nothing else. At the civilian hospital, packed with the hundreds of casualties from the two days of bombing by the US Ninth Air Force, an American truck drove up. It brought a load of Red Cross Christmas presents, which the men of the 120th Infantry, who had fought at the side of the Engineers, had donated to local children injured in the raids.

The five American soldiers who had brought the presents were first clapped by the wards of injured children, packed in tight in white-painted metal beds. Then they were ushered into another room, which was lit solely by candles.

A little bewildered they stood there, twisting their helmets helplessly, while the nuns, who acted as nursing sisters, knelt and began to sing 'Silent Night', in German.

The soldiers cried.

Outside the shattered town two of Skorzeny's men, both volunteers, crept down the hill that led from 'Five Corners'. They were going to bring in dead comrades.

Silently the two men moved to where the wrecked half-track and American armoured car marked the scene of the massacre. All around were snowy mounds which showed the places where their comrades had been mowed down by the Americans. They cleared the snow from one body and tried to lift the corpse, but the body was frozen to the ground. They set to work with their knives chipping away the ice to free the body, which they carried to a waiting jeep hidden beyond the rise.

Thereafter they returned for another and another, stacking them like cordwood in the back of the jeep, always getting closer to the American positions. The men worked on. Suddenly, just as they had freed yet another body and were lugging it towards the jeep, there was the crunch of a boot on the hard snow. They froze. The noise came closer. Dark shapes appeared out of the night. The two men found themselves staring into the faces of an American patrol, waiting for the first angry challenge to be followed by the shots which would surely kill them.

Nothing happened. The Americans took another look at the two Germans, then proceeded silently on their way, like neighbours passing each other in the night.

The two Germans felt an overwhelming sense of brotherhood. It was Christmas Eve and they were, Americans and Germans, one in Christ. As they dragged the last body to the jeep, a grenade shot from where the Americans had disappeared, hissed into the air to explode in a burst of red flame like a star to light their way home.

Up at Ligneuville, which was under constant American fire, with the windows of his quarters rattling, Otto Skorzeny spent his last Christmas Eve in freedom for some time to come. (Like Giskes, von der Heydte and the rest of those involved in the great deception, he would be behind bars on Christmas Eve, 1945.) He drank wine given him by the local priest and ate a piece of beef taken from a cow killed by gunfire that morning and prepared by one of Hauptmann Stielau's men, who had been a naval cook.

Skorzeny had already made his decision. As soon as he had recovered his sight, he would volunteer for a front-line assignment in the East. The West was lost. Although the Führer still might have grandiose plans for the continuation of the great offensive in the Ardennes, Skorzeny knew that they had lost the initiative. They would never break through to the Meuse now.

Some 20 miles away Obersturmbannführer Jochen Peiper, who, with Skorzeny, was to have led that great drive, had already come to the same conclusion. Leaving behind a fifty-man suicide squad, his badly wounded, and their American prisoners at La Gleize, he set out with the remaining 800 of his original 5,000 men on a bold cross-country trek through American lines in an attempt to reach their own.

With him he had a captured American battalion commander, Hal McCown of the 30th Infantry Division. Major McCown related later how they marched most of the twenty-fourth, without any food. McCown, carrying only an empty canteen, didn't know how the young SS men kept up, laden as they were with all their weapons, including mortars and machine guns, as they slogged up and down the steep, snowbound hillsides.

Once a soldier dropped to his knees and was threatened by an officer, 'If you fall behind you will be shot!' The man crawled on on hands and knees. Several times, while Skorzeny ate a traditional German Christmas Eve meal, the defeated command had confused skirmishes with paratroopers of the US 82nd Airborne Division who were holding the line.

At midnight, when McCown thought that not only he himself but also the young SS men could not go on any longer, 'suddenly tracer bullets flashed all around us and we could hear the machine-gun bullets cutting the trees very close over us,' he recalled afterwards. 'I could hear commands being shouted in both German and English.' He realised that he was right in the middle of an American position and that this was his chance to escape.

He dropped to the ground and started crawling away from the stalled Germans. After 100 yards he stood up. Whistling a popular tune as loudly as possible, he strode towards the US lines.

McCown had reached the lines of the 82nd Airborne, but before he could blurt out his story to the airborne troopers, Peiper and his SS men had vanished. McCown would not see Peiper again until their roles had been reversed, with the German the prisoner and he the captor.

As for Jochen Peiper, he fell asleep for nearly twenty-four hours, 'but as I did so, I knew it was all over. We'd lost . . . not only the Battle of the Ardennes, but also the war.'*

Hitler was still not convinced. At five minutes after midnight on 1 January 1945, he spoke over the radio to the German people. Confidently he cried into the microphone:

> Our people are resolved to fight the war to victory under any and all circumstances. . . . The world must know that this state will never capitulate. . . . Germany will rise like a phoenix from its ruined cities and this will go down in history as the miracle of the twentieth century!
>
> I want, therefore, at this hour, as spokesman of Greater Germany, to promise solemnly to the Almighty that we shall fulfil our duty faithfully and unshakeably in the New Year, too, in the firm belief that the hour will strike when victory will ultimately come to him who is most worthy of it, *the Greater German Reich!*

---

* Related to the author

Bold words indeed, with the Ardennes counter-attack beginning to peter out and with the Russians in the East preparing to launch their final offensive against the Reich! But once again Hitler was preparing to surprise the Western Allies, just as he had done on 16 December 1944.

Exactly 7¾ hours after General Patton, the 'Liberator of Bastogne', had ordered every available gun in his half-a-million-strong Third Army to fire a salute to the New Year, the year of victory, nearly 1,000 Messerschmitt 109s and Focke Wulfs 190s took off from snow-covered fields all over the Rhineland. Grouped in four large wings, observing absolute radio silence (again Ultra let the Allied side down), they flew westwards, guided by a lone Junkers 88. As they approached the front, the Junkers turned back, and now they were directed to their targets, just as von der Heydte's Junkers had been, by coloured smoke, searchlights and the 'Christmas Trees', the golden rain, multiple-flares.

At 0805 hours, a tiny Taylorcraft artillery-spotting aircraft, which carried no weapons, was flying over the Allied front when it spotted part of the aerial armada. The pilot radioed back a frantic message: *'Have just passed formation of at least 200 Messerschmitts flying low on course 320!'*

It was the first indication to the Allied High Command that Hitler had surprised them again.

On the previous night, virtually every fighter pilot in the Reich had been placed on alert, forbidden to drink and ordered to go to bed early. There would be no long-drawn-out New Year's Eve celebration this year. At five the pilots were awakened, given real bean coffee instead of the usual ersatz, bars of the specially drug-enriched chocolate (handed out to pilots to fight off fatigue) and were told their mission.

German intelligence had worked out the locations of every Allied air base, and now every pilot was given a large-scale map on which these bases were clearly marked, together with return course, landmarks and detailed routing instructions. They were going to 'take out' every one of those bases. The plan was met by wild enthusiasm, and Goering added to it by doing a lightning tour of all the squadrons which were to take part in the greatest German aerial attack since the Battle of Britain four long years before.

Now, in three new groupings, they broke up and began their surprise attack: The first was to fly the length of the Zuider Zee, skimming the water and beaches to hit Brussels Airport. The next was to come in at ground level through Arnhem down as far as Eindhoven. And the third was to fly over Venlo to debouch along the line of forward American Army Air Corps bases.

In every case they achieved almost total surprise. General Freddie de Guingand, Montgomery's Chief-of-Staff, was holding his usual morning conference that New Year's Day, when one of his staff broke in with, 'These aircraft are dropping things on the town.'

De Guingand didn't think much of it. There were always aircraft, naturally Allied, taking off and landing at Brussels Airport. Suddenly there was a great roar. A plane zoomed across at the field at tree-top height. 'Christ, it's a 190!' someone yelled in alarm.

De Guingand recalled later, 'I'm afraid there was a break in my conference as we went out to see what was happening. Bombs and cannon fire were to be heard and the air was full of German aircraft circling round and round and then diving down to shoot up the aircraft on Brussels airfield. Columns of black smoke were rising from that area and, sad to say, there was not a single British plane about.'

Later after the Germans had gone, he went out to survey the damage; it was tremendous. At Brussels/Evere, 123 transport aircraft, Flying Fortresses, Typhoons and Spitfires were destroyed.

It was no different at the big field at Eindhoven where the Canadian Typhoon Wing and the Polish Spitfire Wing were virtually destroyed. Everywhere the Germans were astonishingly successful, catching the Allied flak and pilots by surprise, with hardly an exception.

At Aschen Field, Belgium, American ace Lieutenant-Colonel John Meyer, with thirty-five and a half kills to his credit, was about to take off for the dawn patrol over St Vith, now in German hands, when a Focke Wulf 190 came roaring in at ground level, barrelling straight for his Mustang.

Meyer knew he didn't have a chance. This was it! Suddenly the radial-engined German fighter broke to the right. It had seen an empty C-47 transport. Its machine guns started to chatter. Bullets ripped the length of the plane. Astounded at his good luck, Meyer zoomed into the sky. With his undercarriage still retracting, he let the Focke Wulf have a burst. The fighter exploded and crashed on to the field, with a pinwheel skid.

There were Germans everywhere now, a wealth of targets to choose from. Meyer picked another Focke Wulf. Every time he got the German in his sights, American flak from the ground slammed into the wings of the Mustang. He found he had a big hole gaping in front of his cockpit. He'd have to land soon – or crash! At last he cornered the elusive German. With the last belt of his ammunition, he shot him right out of the sky. Within a matter of minutes he had achieved two 'kills'.

In the end some thirty-six Germans were shot down by pilots who managed to get airborne, while the flak accounted for another fifty-seven. By 10.30 that morning it was all over, and nearly one hundred German planes had been put out of action. But they had succeeded in wrecking 300 Allied planes and knocking out twenty-seven Allied bases from Brussels to Eindhoven. Goering's 'Big Blow', as the operation was code-named, had been an astonishing success, brilliantly worked out and superbly executed.

Immediately there was a cover-up in the Allied camp. De Guingand was typical when he wrote, 'But although a great deal of damage had been sustained, we could afford it, whilst the enemy could not stand the cost of his audacious attack. His losses amounted to over 200 aircraft, which meant a great enemy defeat.'*

Those who had borne the brunt of the attack were not so sanguine. French fighter ace Pierre Clostermann, whose wing, based at Voekel, Holland, had been in the air at the time of the attack, wrote later: 'The American censorship and the Press service, in a flat spin, tried to present this attack as a

---

* Later it was claimed that 300 German fighter pilots, including fifty-nine leaders, had been killed in the two-hour attack.

great Allied victory by publishing peculiar figures. We pilots were still laughing about them three months later.'

In fact, at a cost of 100 aircraft, the Germans succeeded in paralysing the Tactical Air Force for more than a week, as well as surprising the complacent Allies. From dawn to dusk, Clostermann's 122nd Wing in effect kept the aerial offensive going, losing eighteen pilots and twenty-three aircraft in sixteen days.

That wasn't the only surprise that Hitler sprang on the West that first day of January 1945. Just before midnight in the area now vacated by Patton's Third Army, which was making a thrust into the Bulge, eight German divisions launched the last enemy attack of the war on the Western front.

Code-named 'North Wind', it hit American and French positions in the Vosges area south of the Ardennes. Later the Americans would claim, just as they had after the surprise air attack on New Year's Day, that they had expected the attack all the time. But it upset them so much that, all the same, contingency plans were made to fall back into the French Maginot Line, that great white elephant of twentieth-century French military planning, and evacuate the Alsatian capital of Strasbourg on the Rhine.

By 2 January, with the Germans pushing hard and civilians already beginning that long trek westwards yet again, General Devers, commanding the US Seventh and the French First Armies in the area, made it clear to the French commander of the city that it might have to be evacuated soon.

There was an immediate outcry from the French. Devers, and naturally Eisenhower, were informed that more than 100,000 inhabitants would have to be evacuated from the city and that another 300,000 to 400,000 civilians in the surrounding area would be subject to German reprisals once the Gestapo took over again.*

A first-class political row erupted. De Gaulle felt that he

---

*Like the Belgian east cantons and Luxembourg, Alsace had been annexed by the Reich in May 1940; therefore any citizen who might have helped the Allies would be regarded as a traitor.

had been betrayed. Why hadn't he been warned of the American contingency plan in advance? He told the Supreme Commander that 'whatever happens the French will defend Strasbourg' – which meant in effect that he would remove French troops from American command and go it alone. As for General Jean de Lattre de Tassigny, the commander of the First French Army under Devers, he complained bitterly that 'the secret of the withdrawal was kept even from our liaison mission'.

Immediately, de Gaulle went over to the counter-offensive. He knew that American generals fought their battles in the limelight of the media and were tremendously concerned about their 'image' in the press 'back home'. He sent Marshal Juin to warn Eisenhower that if he sacrificed Alsace in order to win back the Ardennes, which he had already conquered once, there would be severe criticism of the Supreme Commander. What would the American public think?

General Bedell Smith, Eisenhower's hot-tempered, red-haired Chief-of-Staff, who always maintained that 'somebody has to be a sonuvabitch around this headquarters', wasn't impressed. Thereupon the big, heavy-nosed French Marshal stated that General de Gaulle had ordered de Lattre to take responsibility for the defence of Strasbourg.

Hotly Smith retorted, 'If that is so, it is bordering on insubordination, pure and simple, and the French army will not get a single further round of ammunition or gallon of petrol.'

Now it was Juin's turn to threaten. 'All right', he snapped, 'in that case, General de Gaulle will forbid American forces the use of French railways and communications.'

While the German attack started to peter out, both in Alsace and the Ardennes, the threat to Strasbourg escalated even further. De Gaulle dispatched telegrams of protest to both Roosevelt, who always compared the Free French leader to a latter-day Joan of Arc, and to Churchill, who maintained that the 'cross of Lorraine' (de Gaulle) was one of his heaviest burdens of the war. Next the French leader got in touch with Eisenhower and arranged a meeting, at which Churchill, who chanced to be in Eisenhower's headquarters, was present. All five accounts* of what happened at that decisive meeting at Versailles on 3 January 1945 are contradictory. A sixth, written by John Eisenhower, the Supreme Commander's son, states that 'Eisenhower's temper, until then known principally only to his immediate staff, flared. He allowed himself the luxury of informing the Provisional President of the French Republic that if [the French were to go it alone], the French Army would get no ammunition, supplies or food unless it obeyed his orders.'

In the end it seems that Churchill managed to smooth over the situation, telling de Gaulle, 'All my life I have known what significance Alsace has had for the French. I agree with General de Gaulle that this fact must be taken into consideration.'

So it was agreed that Strasbourg should not be evacuated. An unpleasant political row had been avoided, but it had been nip-and-tuck. And as Operation 'North Wind' finally floundered in the deep snows of the Vosges, Hitler was unaware that his last surprise operation in the West had almost brought about that political split he was always trying to bring about among the four disparate Allies.

Although the German attackers never got closer than 8 miles to Strasbourg, it was clear that the constant surprises and scares of the last three weeks had taken their toll. Eisenhower had lost his nerve. Indeed, some of his intimates, such as Kay Summersby and General Hughes, thought he was a very sick man on the verge of a nervous breakdown.

In that first week of January, he decided to appeal for help to Marshal Stalin, the Russian dictator. He planned to send his deputy, Air Marshal Tedder, personally to Moscow, but bad weather delayed the flight. So on 6 January Churchill volunteered to appeal for him. He wrote to Stalin as follows:

> The battle in the west is very heavy and at times large decisions may be called for from the Supreme Command. . . . It is Eisenhower's great desire and need to know in outline what you plan to do. . . . I shall be grateful if you can tell me whether we

---

* Those of Churchill, Eisenhower, General de Gaulle, Marshal Juin and Field Marshal Alan Brooke.

can count on a major Russian offensive on the Vistula front or elsewhere during January with any other plans you may care to mention. I shall not pass this most secret information to anyone except Field Marshal Brooke and General Eisenhower and only under the conditions of the utmost secrecy. I regard the matter as urgent.

Two days later Stalin answered:

We are preparing to take the offensive, but the weather is at present unfavourable. Nevertheless taking into account the position of our Allies on the Western Front, GHQ of the Supreme Command has decided to accelerate the completion of our preparation and, regardless of the weather, to commence large-scale operations against the Germans along the whole Central Front not later than the second half of January.

Eisenhower had his offensive!
On the same day that Churchill received his answer from Stalin, 8 January 1945, Hitler at last ordered the withdrawal from the Ardennes. What was left of his battered Sixth SS Panzer Army would move east now to meet the new threat – and would fail to stop it. Hitler might have surprised Eisenhower in the Ardennes, but he would not surprise 'Uncle Joe', whose agents in the Reich already knew Hitler's intentions.* If anyone was going to emerge victor from that secret war, conducted by the three colonels in the Ardennes, it would be, ironically enough, the Russians.

2

On 15 May 1945, more than a week after the surrender of the German forces to the Allies, three men in the uniform of the SS, all fully armed, led by a tall man in the uniform of a general, walked down the sun-baked mountain roads into the

---

*Throughout the winter of 1944–45, the Russians were steadily parachuting agents into Germany's eastern provinces.

Austrian city of Salzburg to surrender to the Americans. The Americans, however, were apparently too busy to receive the surrender. The division to which they reported was being moved and they had prisoners enough. These days generals were a dime a dozen. Indeed, the massive general officer was hauled away by a GI to help him buy a bottle of wine at a local *Weinstube*. He then offered the general a drink, saying happily, 'Drink you guys, tonight you'll hang!'

At last, after much seemingly aimless driving around, the general found someone to whom he could surrender his unit, which was still apparently free and in hiding in the Alps above Salzburg. He also introduced himself as Otto Skorzeny, commander of an SS Jagdkommando.

In an instant, the GIs' bored, casual attitude vanished. Skorzeny was ordered to give up his weapon and take a seat. Suddenly his hands were handcuffed behind his back, a machine gun thrust through the open window, with guards appearing from nowhere.

Half an hour later, after being stripped and searched for the same kind of L-Pill with which he had equipped his jeep-team men in what now seemed another age, he was taken by jeep, covered by US armoured cars, to meet the press. They were all there, eager to meet the 'most dangerous man in Europe'.

'Skorzeny certainly looks the part,' wrote the female correspondent of the *New York Times* later. 'He is striking in a tough way: a huge powerful figure. The "Beast of Belsen" is something out of a nursery in comparison.' And for the sake of her female readers, presumably, she gushed, 'He has blue eyes.'

A British correspondent present wrote, 'It was thought better to keep Skorzeny with his hands manacled behind his back. When he was given a cigarette, it was lit and he had to have the ash shaken off. A glass of water was held to his lips.'

Chicago read the next day that the interview in far-off Austria had ended 'with the clicking of pistols as MPs prepared for what might happen next'. And New York's *Daily News* correspondent ended his account by writing: 'I'll say this. He was a true Nazi throughout. He walked out with his head high – and with a flock of American soldiers wishing he would make just one dash for freedom.'

In spite of the gushing prose and the attempts at human interest, there was one question posed at that first press conference that made Skorzeny uneasy and was going to plague him for nearly two years to come: it was that 'damned Café de la Paix business'.

'Why did you try to murder General Eisenhower?'

'I didn't,' Skorzeny replied promptly. 'If I had ever been ordered to attack Allied GHQ, I should have made a plan to do so. If I had made a plan, I would have carried it out. And no one would have been left in doubt of what I was trying to do.'

That was that. As the *New York Times* wrote the next day, 'Handsome despite the scar that stretched from ear to chin, Skorzeny smilingly disclaimed credit for leading the mission to murder members of the Supreme Command.' As the last of the three colonels was led off into captivity, it was clear that no one believed his denials.

Colonel Giskes was arrested almost immediately the war ended. Naturally, he was high on the list of Abwehr officers that the British Secret Intelligence Service wanted to question. After a preliminary interrogation about his role in the 'North Pole' Operation, which was soon going to be the subject of a major enquiry by the Dutch Parliament (and an embarrassment for the British government, as it turned out), he was flown to England. There he was imprisoned at Latchmere House, a three-storey manor house, hidden by a high wall, in the Surrey village of Ham Common.

Under the command of a bemonocled Rhodesian colonel nicknamed 'Tin-Eye' Stephens, a skilled staff put through their paces Giskes and those of his agents (including 'Freddy', the Austrian who had penetrated the Churchill family) who were still alive and could be apprehended.

According to Colonel Giskes, he was often subjected to harsh and humiliating treatment there, being brought from the centre's 'cage' (it is still there) to the manor house itself, where he was stripped naked, the classic manner of cutting an important prisoner down to size, and faced with hours-long interrogation by relays of SIS men. One of the SIS's main interests was, of course, Operation 'North Pole' and how it was that forty-two SOE agents had been executed. At least, this is what Giskes thought at the time; later, after he had been interrogated by the Dutch, who maintained that perhaps the SIS had sacrificed their SOE agents for their own purposes, he suspected that his SIS interrogators were really after how much he knew of *their* operations in Holland, while Blunt's agents were falling so easily into German hands.

Giskes opened up. He told the British all he knew. He knew that his life was at stake if he didn't. Finally he was able to prove that he had made appeals to Berlin for the captive agents' lives to be spared, and the subject of 'North Pole' was dropped by his interrogators.

The time passed leadenly, with ever new interrogations and enquiries. One day, however, he heard a voice that he had last heard at the Hôtel Dom in Cologne six years before during the course of his attempts to wind up the 'Z-Ring', the SIS's main continental spy network. He risked a glance at the courtyard below and recognised the owner of that voice. It was Hooper, the double traitor, who had once attempted to kill him. Now Hooper sported the pips of a captain in the British army!

Years later, Giskes recalled: 'I was not prepared to betray anyone. But Hooper was different. I was still angry with him.' The next time Giskes was run through his paces by his interrogator about the Z-Ring, he revealed that his contact within the SIS had been Hooper. Immediately he was asked to identify the traitor. He did so willingly.

A month later, when he was again brought to the main house, he asked his interrogator what had happened to Hooper. The answer was a laconic 'We've hanged him!'

Finally Giskes was released, without ever having mentioned Operation 'Hermann' and how he had successfully fooled the Americans over the true intentions of Dietrich's Sixth SS Panzer Army in the Ardennes. Middle-aged and with no career to speak of, Giskes drifted back into his old *métier*. He began to work for the shadowy spy master General Gehlen, who had once been Hitler's Chief-of-Eastern-Intelligence and had at the end of the war immediately attempted to place his unrivalled knowledge of the Red army, as well as his organisation, at the disposal of the erstwhile Russian ally, the American army.

For a while no one wanted the services of the *Organisation Gehlen*, as it was soon to be known, until at last, ironically enough, the man whom Giskes had fooled so effectively in December 1944, Bradley's Chief-of-Intelligence, General Sibert, took him up and recommended him to Washington. Gehlen was smuggled out of Germany and by 1947 was running his spy service for the benefit of the newly created CIA. Thus it was that when Giskes was finally released and began working again, his first employer was none other than the general he'd helped to scare so badly that black Christmas – General Bedell Smith!*

Baron von der Heydte was the first of the three colonels to be released from Allied captivity. As he had convinced the Americans that he had had nothing to do with the Skorzeny operation, the only obstacle to his release was whether he or the men under his command had committed any war crimes. The New Zealand and Australian forces, as well as the British, were contacted to check out his record as a battalion commander in Crete, as were the Americans of the 101st Airborne against whom he had fought in Normandy. All their replies were negative. Now the Belgian authorities were approached.

In 1945 under the leadership of the Prince Regent, the civilian authorities of that country were conducting a major enquiry into the events of December 1944 to January 1945 in the Ardennes. There had been hundreds of reports of indiscriminate shootings by German soldiers as they had swept westwards; and, naturally, the American army was making its own investigations about what had taken place at that notorious 'Five Corners' of Baugnez. Again, the Belgians turned in a negative report. Baron von der Heydte could be released from the POW camp; his record was clean.

Duly his release took place, and the good Baron was

---

* The first head of the CIA. Another, much more unsavoury character recruited into the same organisation was the 'Butcher of Lyons', Klaus Barbie

'de-nazified', as was customary in those days (though later some critics thought he was not such an anti-Nazi as he claimed). With no German army in existence, von der Heydte resumed his old academic career, the one he had abandoned to go – as he said – into the 'inner emigration' of the professional army. He rose rapidly up the promotion ladder to become Professor of Law at the University of Würzburg and, once the West German Bundeswehr had been established, no less than a Herr General der Reserve. That December, when a drunken Dietrich had taunted him with his 'damned pigeons', but when he had insisted on a demarcation between his own force and that of Skorzeny, had paid dividends, handsome ones. For while von der Heydte was already taking his first steps in becoming accepted by the post-war German establishment, the commanders for whom and at whose side he had fought that black Christmas were now fighting not only for their freedom but for their lives: the SS were on trial.

All of them were there at Dachau – Dietrich, Kraemer, Priess, naturally Peiper, and, of course, Skorzeny. Bitterly they, and the rest of the one-million-strong Waffen SS, spoke of themselves as being the *'Alibi der Nation'*: they thought they were to be condemned to prove the innocence of the so-called 'good Germans'. And condemned they were for the events of that December in the Ardennes.

Just after dawn on 16 July 1946, Jochen Peiper was ordered to his feet and led into the court where a panel of military judges waited for him. General Dalbey, the president of the court, held the verdict in his hand, which he now began to read out, pausing only for a moment before he read out the sentence to the prisoner standing rigidly to attention in his old German uniform, stripped of all insignia and badges of rank. It was death by hanging.

'Tod durch Erhängen', the interpreter said softly.

Peiper didn't need his services; he spoke fluent English. The 30-year-old SS colonel opened his lips. For an instance there was an absolute silence. Then the word came. It was audible right to the last row of the court. *'Danke!'* Peiper snapped and turning smartly, marched out.

That morning seventy-four sentences were passed for what had happened in the Ardennes that black Christmas, with two minutes allotted to each. They ranged from life for Dietrich, the oldest accused man present, through death for forty-three of the seventy-four, to life for the youngest man at Dachau, Fritz Gebauer, who had been sixteen in December 1944.

As the prosecutor, Colonel Ellis, told the press, while the rest of the northern hemisphere was still eating breakfast, 'They [the accused] showed no more emotion than if they had been eating a meal. They marched in, snapped to attention, listened to their sentences and then did an about-face and marched off.'

The Malmédy killers had been dealt with. Now it was Otto Skorzeny's turn.

A lot had happened to the scar-faced giant since he had surrendered to the American authorities. Much of his former confidence in himself, the Party big shots and his fellow officers had vanished. Almost immediately he had been grilled for six hours by Colonel Sheen, (who had ordered the 'imprisonment' of Eisenhower) about Skorzeny's exact plans respecting the person of the Supreme Commander. He had been accused of war crimes. He had played a minor role in the Nuremburg Trials, and the prosecution had tried to gain him as a witness in the case against the Malmédy killers.

In December 1946, Skorzeny fell ill; he spent a terrible winter in the so-called 'Bunker' at Dachau, where 300 other Germans waited to be tried as war criminals. He heard in May 1947 that he was going to be put on trial for war crimes, and in August of that year he was informed that he was specifically accused of having 'conspired to ill-treat, torture and kill at least a hundred American prisoners of war' during the Battle of the Bulge.

On 18 August 1947, after two years behind bars, Skorzeny and nine other officers of the Panzerbrigade 150 were put on trial, being defended by Lieutenant-Colonel Robert Durst, a former American cavalry officer. To defend suspected Nazi war criminals in the year 1947 was a very bold thing for an American officer to do, and Durst grilled Skorzeny for four days – 'the hardest grilling I ever underwent' – before he was finally convinced of his client's innocence. He told Skorzeny, smiling for the first time since they had been introduced, 'I am sure of your innocence on every charge. Now I know you have nothing to hide, I will fight for you as if you were my brother.'

There were four charges levelled against Skorzeny and the others, including stealing US Red Cross parcels, but it was really one charge only, that they had shot captured US prisoners, which concerned Colonel Durst. Where this alleged massacre had taken place Skorzeny never found out, but he reasoned that because one of his jeep teams had been with Peiper, he was somehow suspected of having played a role in the Malmédy Massacre.

The trial dragged on. Back in his prison, Skorzeny met a Polish officer who had been arrested for spying for the Russians. As the camp's guards were Poles, the Polish officer had the run of the place. He suggested he should make a break and take Skorzeny with him. The latter refused, believing the Pole couldn't make it. Three days later he was gone, leaving Skorzeny behind.

Three young American officers smuggled themselves into Skorzeny's cell. They volunteered to testify that American soldiers had shot German prisoners during the Battle of the Bulge. Skorzeny turned them down, saying that 'two wrongs didn't make a right.'

But if his ex-enemies were helpful, his fellow-countrymen were not. His former supply officer gave evidence against Skorzeny. A German general who had listed all the Allied breaches of international law during the war was asked to give evidence for Skorzeny. He refused. Radl, Skorzeny's long-time adjutant who had surrendered with him that May, appeared for the prosecution in a minor role. The Malmédy murderers, most of them awaiting the rope, also gave evidence for the other side, save Peiper, who stated categorically that he had been forced to appear and had nothing to say.

Finally Skorzeny himself was put into the witness box. Here he stayed for two days, detailing his role in the Battle of the Bulge and skirting around the tricky business of wearing American uniforms. Once Durst asked Skorzeny about the plan to kill Eisenhower.

It was the 'damned Café de la Paix' business all over again, but before Skorzeny could explain how it had all started, the president of the court ruled the question out of order. So that particular *canard* was allowed to fly for many a year to come.

The uniform business came up again. Skorzeny detailed the many uses the Allies had made of German uniform before his own men dressed in American clothing. He recalled that British officers had been captured in German uniform in Hungary, for example, and had not been shot. As late as the summer of 1944, Poles had dressed in German uniform during the Warsaw uprising and had also not been shot. The Americans, too, had used German uniform at Aachen and at Saarlautern, three months after the Battle of the Bulge was over.

It was after the almost day-long discussion of the legality of using enemy uniforms in battle that Colonel Durst, like a magician, pulled 'a rabbit' out of the hat. He announced he had a witness for the defence, 'Wing-Commander Forrest Yeo-Thomas'. Moments later a short, sturdy figure in the faded blue of the Royal Air Force walked to the witness chair, sat down and looked at the nine American officers of the panel who stared at this British flier in astonishment; what did he have to do with Skorzeny? For his part, Skorzeny, equally surprised, noted that the little Englishman bore many ribbons for gallantry on his chest, including the George Cross.

Swiftly Durst, who loved surprises, explained who the little Englishman was: none other than one of the Secret Service's leading agents, who had parachuted into France to organise the SIS's networks there. Under the code-name 'White Rabbit' he had escaped capture many times until he was finally betrayed and sent to Buchenwald. He had escaped from the concentration camp, leaving a corpse in his place, and walked through Germany until finally he had reached the American lines. But after the war he had returned and ensured that twenty-two of his former guards were executed for murdering prisoners at Buchenwald: hardly the man, some of his listeners must have thought, to help Otto Skorzeny, whom Yeo-Thomas had never previously met.

Soon, however, as the Englishman gave his testimony, it

became clear why Durst had called him for the defence. Without hesitation Yeo-Thomas explained:

> My comrade was in prison at Rennes in Brittany. I reconnoitred the gaol and bribed one of the guards to find out when the rounds were made and the general procedure. . . . Then I put some of my men who spoke German into German uniform and secured copies of German papers required to take a prisoner out of gaol. We stole a German car and I also had a van rigged up to resemble a prison van. . . .

Durst let the little Englishman talk, knowing that the panel could not help but see the resemblance between this operation and Skorzeny's 'Trojan Horse' operation and would draw their own conclusions.

> The men in German uniforms, one of them disguised as an officer, were to go into the guardroom. If the prisoner were not delivered to us on sight of the papers, if there were any hesitation, we would dispose of the guards quickly and silently.

Yeo-Thomas let his words and their significance sink in. Now Colonel Durst spoke at last: 'Did you obtain German uniforms for this purpose?' he asked.

'Yes.'

'How were they obtained?'

'The details I could not tell you. I gave instructions to obtain uniforms by hook or by crook.'

The panel didn't need to be told how Yeo-Thomas's agents had secured German uniforms in wartime France; there was only one way they could have done so.

Finally Durst put his main question: 'To prevent discovery [of their plot] what would the practice be?'

Wing-Commander Yeo-Thomas looked around before answering. Then he said softly, 'Bump off the other guy.'

The prosecution's case had vanished. Now Yeo-Thomas buried it deeply for good, maintaining that the Allies had done the same sort of things as Skorzeny.

The court had either to acquit him or declare that there was one law for the victor and another for the vanquished. The rules of the kind of war he and Skorzeny had conducted were kill or be killed. 'Bump off the other guy. If you come out of it – a medal perhaps and no questions asked. If you don't – too bad!'

That was that. Yeo-Thomas had explained as well as any one could the changing rules of clandestine warfare. Now it was up to the prosecution.

Durst turned to his opposite number, Colonel Rosenfeld, who had been a security officer during the Battle of the Bulge. The prosecutor shook his head. He had no questions to ask. He knew he had no case now.

As Yeo-Thomas stepped down, Skorzeny snapped a quick order, '*Stillgestanden!*' The other nine clicked to attention, and Skorzeny bowed to the little Englishman. It was the only token of respect and thanks that they were able to offer the former enemy who had saved them.

Skorzeny was transferred to an open camp, where he helped the US Army Historical Division to prepare an account of the Mussolini rescue. After that it was back to the cells. He went 'on strike' for better conditions and got them. Christmas 1948 came and he was still in prison, three years after that fateful December. Spring came, and Skorzeny was transferred to a German prison, for soon the new Federal Republic was to emerge. He was allowed out to work on the city of Darmstadt's 'Rubble Express', clearing away the ruins of the bombing. Nearly a year after his acquittal he was still in prison because the German authorities would not 'de-nazify' him, a prerequisite for a civilian existence in the new democratic Germany. He wrote to Yeo-Thomas explaining his plight. 'What should he do?'

The ex-spy chief's answer from Paris, where he was now a director of Molyneux, the dressmaker's, was laconic and to the point. It was '*Escape!*'

On 27 July 1948, Otto Skorzeny did just that. He stowed away in the boot of a car leaving the Darmstadt camp, his former adjutant, Radl, convulsed with laughter, tried to squeeze his gigantic frame inside while four fellow-prisoners shielded them. One day later he was in the high mountains near Berchtesgaden, where once he had attempted to set up the 'Last Redoubt', for that last-ditch stand of Hitler's leaders. Now they were all dead, by their own hand, or on the gallows. He was free at last!

A battle does not end when the echoes of the last shots have died away into the surrounding hills, and the last cry of pain or anger has subsided. Just as when a stone is thrown into a pond and the ripples spread ever outwards, as if they could on for ever, it is the same with a great battle.

For some it means tortured nightmares, clothes bathed in sweat, the bed rumpled, as the feverish cries, the appeals for help, the curses, the commands echo and re-echo down the dark, endless corridors of the mind.

For others it means bitter accusations and counter-accusations, the permanent souring of the personality, as the old battles are fought and re-fought, with that eternal, over-whelming question being raised time and time again 'Where did I go wrong?'

Ten years after Skorzeny made his escape, fleeing to Spain, and Giskes and von der Heydte were long re-established in West Germany, that once handsome young SS colonel for whom all their effort had been made, Jochen Peiper, still languished in gaol. Thanks to many well-wishers, including the notorious Joe McCarthy, his sentence had been reduced from death to life imprisonment.

Just before Christmas 1958, he was finally released into a world that he knew no more. His old comrades, including Dietrich, were all there to meet him. But they met a changed Peiper, soured, bitter, living in the past, a man who felt betrayed by the time – and by his comrades who had adapted so well to the Germany of the 'hard D-Mark' and the 'Eco-nomic Miracle'.

The past was dead, fit only for beer-bellied, ageing chauvin-ists to argue about at their *Stammtisch* in the local tavern; and the future held no great interest for a man who knew nothing but war.

He tried. He 'got on the steeplechase for money', as he called it bitterly. But the past would not leave him in peace. He lost his job with Porsche because the many Italian 'guest-workers', as the West German euphemism had it, would not work for a man who had been accused of war crimes in Italy.

He tried again with a publishing firm in Stuttgart. Again the past caught up with him in the shape of John Toland's book on the Battle of the Bulge, and the movie *The Battle of the Bulge* in which Robert Shaw played Peiper. He was summoned to the local public prosecutor's office, where again he was accused of war crimes. His new-found friends in the Swabian city dropped him like a hot brick.

Now he was approaching sixty. His hair was grey and plastered down in the style of his class in the thirties; his neck was scrawny and too small for his collar. He seemed to have shrunk. But he was as aggressive and bitter as in the old days.

'You know that tank of mine at La Gleize,' he said. 'I'd like to drag the damn thing here to Stuttgart and put it outside that entrance overnight and see the looks on the faces of the stuffy local citizens next morning. That'd show 'em!'

'I'm sitting on a powder keg, you know. Ellis,* Kemper† and Wiesenthal – they've all tried to get me in the past. One day someone will come along with another "story" and the powder keg will explode under me. Then it'll be over at last!'‡

On 21 June 1976 it was all over. Eight years previously Peiper had left Germany and moved to France, where he had built himself a wooden house in the village of Traves. There he had lived in self-imposed exile translating military books from German into English and vice versa. Apparently *l'Allemand*, as he was called by the locals, was at peace with himself at last. On that June day, the villagers were startled to find their streets smeared with swastikas, SS runes and the name 'Peiper'. A little later a van-load of Communists appeared, distributing pamphlets calling on the villagers to demonstrate against the 'Nazi war cimininal'.

Peiper went to the police. He was told that the local Prefect was under pressure to expel him from France. A little later, in the first week of July, he received his final warning – anonymously, naturally: 'We've warned you often enough –

---

* Colonel Ellis, who prosecuted Peiper at Dachau
† Dr R. Kemper, a prosecutor at Nuremberg
‡ To the author

take off! But you're still here. Now you've only yourself to thank for what is going to happen to you.'

Peiper sent his wife and daughter back to Munich. He refused to go, but he did write a letter to the West German ambassador in Paris, Sigismund von Braun (brother of the missile expert) appealing for help. But by the time von Braun received it, it was already too late.

Bastille Day, 1976, was burningly hot in France. On the nearby *autoroute* heading south, drivers stripped and women wore their bikinis in their cars. Everywhere engines overheated and vehicles broke down as temperatures soared.

Like the rest of France, Traves celebrated the storming of the Bastille, that symbol of revolution. But the sixty-three people of the one-street hamlet were mostly farmers who had to be up early in the morning to milk their cows. By midnight the one café was closed and most of the natives were in bed.

At midnight the shooting started. For a while the locals took them to be fireworks. When the 'fireworks' persisted, and someone spotted flames coming from the direction of *l'Allemand's* house, the fire brigade was alerted. The voluntary firemen tumbled out of their beds and stumbled down to the *pompiers'* shed. They were in for a surprise. Their hoses had been slashed! Finally the police were called.

The gendarmerie in their smart khaki summer uniform arrived at dawn. Too late. It was all over. Poking around in the smoking wreckage of Peiper's house, they found a horrible charred 'thing'. It was Peiper's body, shrunken to a black mummified pygmy by the tremendous heat. Beside it there was a hunting rifle and a Colt, both empty. Jochen Peiper had died as he had lived, fighting to the last, executed thirty-two years after the crime he had committed at that crossroads, once known as 'Five Corners'.

It was the last surprise.

An Afterword

For those interested in such things there is little visible evidence left of that secret war in the Ardennes of forty years ago. Travel up the frontier road that leads into Belgium from Losheim and at Lanzerath you'll find still the Café Palm, almost the same as it was that midnight when Peiper burst into it to find it filled with snoring paras and wounded Amis, telling himself that the 'front had gone to sleep'.

A few miles further east, there is the rebuilt Café Bodarwé, run by Madame's son Louis, and opposite, at the place once known as 'Five Corners', the memorial to the victims of the Massacre, now overshadowed by a hideous blue factory.

Take the same road as Skorzeny's men did on that night when Operation 'Trojan Horse' met its doom, and you'll find a rebuilt Malmédy, the scars of war long vanished save for the bullet-pocked wall of the house where Colonel Pergrim first heard Virgil Lary stutter out his tearful tale of what had happened at 'Five Corners'.

Beyond, on the heights from which von der Heydte's paras came down, some unknown person had erected a cross these many years ago at the exact site of their DZ. It still stands there, weathered and worn by that cold wind, which blows up there winter and summer, as does the wall at Henri Chapelle where Skorzeny's jeep team died with the echoes of *Stille Nacht* ringing in their ears.

Further west on the road that Peiper took, if you grub around in the forests, you'll find the mouldering 75mm shell cases with the date '1944' stamped on their bases, or the shattered bit of rusty metal with a foot-long wooden handle

which falls to bits as soon as you touch it – a German stick
grenade left behind by one of those desperate young men in
the camouflaged tunic of the SS who today is old and white-
haired and tame – if he survived.

A trace here, a trace there. But it is only when you drive
down the church road into the hamlet of La Gleize that you
can feel once again the power and the dread of that dark
December. For there it stands as massive and as menacing as
it did that Saturday, 16 December 1944, when it had first
rumbled across the frontier to commence that bold adven-
ture: Obersturmbannführer Jochen Peiper's last surviving
Tiger tank.

Bibliography

The material for this story has been collected over many years, and many individuals of different nationalities have helped me to obtain it. Sadly, too many of them are dead now. But I would like to thank in particular Sir Kenneth Strong, Group-Captain F. Winterbotham, Field Marshal Templar, Colonel John Eisenhower, H. le Joly, Colonel Ralph Hill, Dr Bouck, Mr Calvin Boykin, General Bruce Clarke, M. K. Fagnoul, M. W. Trees – and the three colonels, Skorzeny, Giskes and Peiper.

Hugh Cole, *The Ardennes: The Battle of the Bulge* (Dept of the Army, Washington).
Dwight D. Eisenhower, *Crusade in Europe* (Doubleday, N.Y.).
John Eisenhower, *The Bitter Woods* (Robert Hale).
Robert B. Merriam, *Dark December* (Ziff–Davis, 1947).
Ronald Lewin, *Ultra Goes to War* (Hutchinson).
John Toland, *The Story of the Bulge* (Random House, N.Y.).
Kriegsschicksale (Doepgen, St Vith).
Jacques Nobecourt, *Le dernier Coup* (Laffont).
J. H. Giles, *The G.I. Journal of Sergeant Giles* (Houghton Mifflin, N.Y.).
J. H. Giles, *Those Damned Engineers* (Houghton Mifflin, N.Y.).
Kay Summersby Morgan, *Past Forgetting* (Collins, London).
———, *Eisenhower Was My Boss* (Dell).
Lothar Greil, *Die Wahrheit unter Malmédy* (Schild Verlag).
Milton Shulman, *Defeat in the West* (Ballantine).
Janusz Piekalkiewics, *Spione, Agenten, Soldaten* (Süd-West Verlag).
Douglas Liversidge, *The Third Front* (Souvenir Press, London).

David Irving, *The War Between the Generals* (Allen Lane, London).

James Gavin, *On to Berlin* (Bantam).

Charles Whiting, *Skorzeny* (Ballantine).

———, *Massacre at Malmédy* (Leo Cooper).

Index